More Grade 4 Piano

16 enjoyable pieces for Grade 4

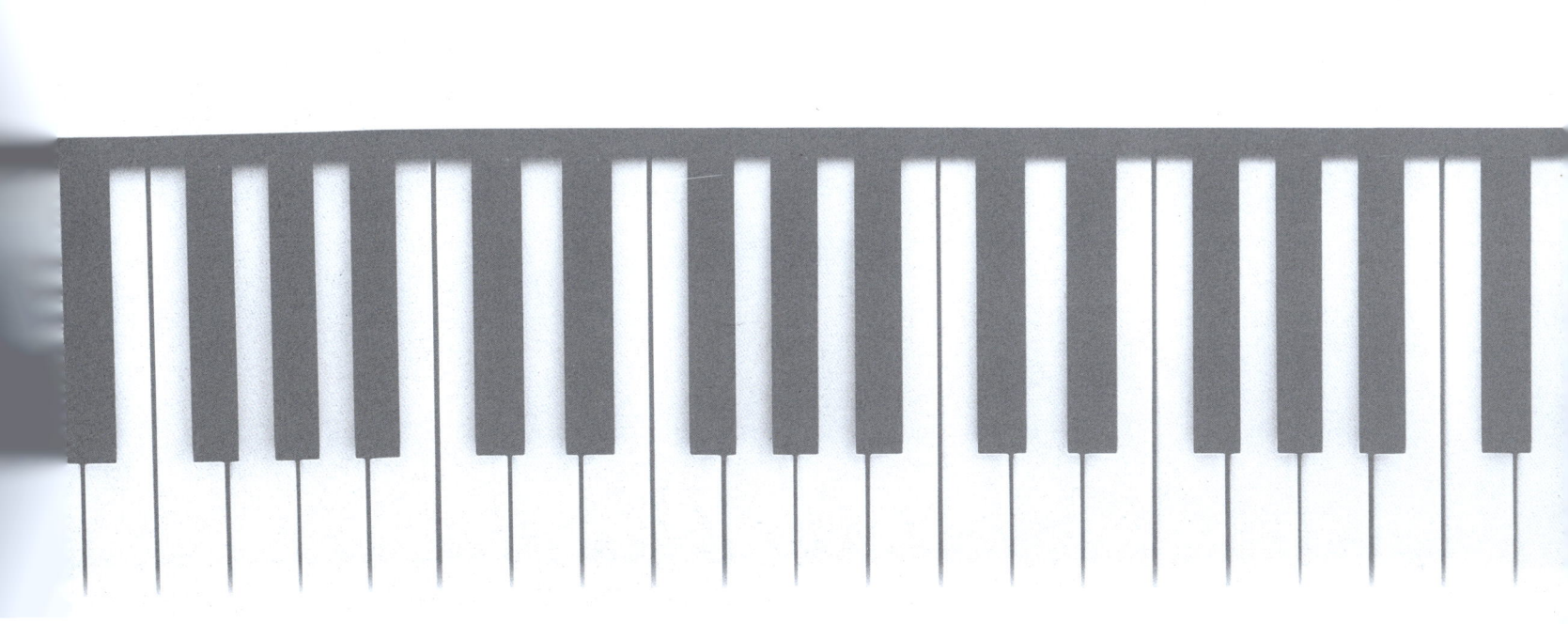

Published by

Chester Music
part of The Music Sales Group
14-15 Berners Street, London W1T 3LJ, UK.

Exclusive Distributors:
Music Sales Limited
Distribution Centre, Newmarket Road,
Bury St Edmunds, Suffolk IP33 3YB, UK.

Music Sales Pty Limited
Level 4, Lisgar House,
30-32 Carrington Street,
Sydney, NSW 2000 Australia.

Order No. CH85272
ISBN 978-1-78558-365-0
This book © Copyright 2017 Chester Music Limited.
All Rights Reserved.

Unauthorised reproduction of any part of this
publication by any means including photocopying
is an infringement of copyright.

Compiled and edited by Sam Lung and James Welland.
Music arranged by Alistair Watson.
Music engraved and processed by Sarah Lofthouse, SEL Music Art Ltd.

Printed in the EU.

Your Guarantee of Quality
As publishers, we strive to produce every book to the
highest commercial standards.
This book has been carefully designed to minimise awkward
page turns and to make playing from it a real pleasure.
Particular care has been given to specifying acid-free, neutral-sized paper
made from pulps which have not been elemental chlorine bleached.
This pulp is from farmed sustainable forests and was
produced with special regard for the environment.
Throughout, the printing and binding have been planned to
ensure a sturdy, attractive publication which should give years of enjoyment.
If your copy fails to meet our high standards,
please inform us and we will gladly replace it.

www.musicsales.com

More Grade 4 Piano Solos

16 enjoyable pieces for Grade 4 pianists

CHESTER MUSIC
PART OF THE MUSIC SALES GROUP
LONDON / NEW YORK / PARIS / SYDNEY / COPENHAGEN / BERLIN / MADRID / HONG KONG / TOKYO

Contents

The Blue Danube Strauss 5

En Bateau Debussy 8

Erla's Waltz Ólafur Arnalds 12

The Family (from *Lore*) Max Richter 15

The Girl From Ipanema 18

Habanera (from *Carmen*) Bizet 20

The James Bond Theme 24

Larghetto (No. 4 from *Les Cinq Doigts*) Stravinsky 28

Lost! Coldplay 30

Over The Rainbow 32

Rolling In The Deep Adele 34

Somewhere Only We Know Lily Allen 36

Song For Gavin Ludovico Einaudi 39

Three Secrets From The Abyss: No. 1 John Harle 42

To A Wild Rose MacDowell 44

Uptown Funk! Mark Ronson feat. Bruno Mars 46

Blue Danube

Music by Johann Strauss

This is a famous waltz by Strauss.
Ask your teacher about the Viennese Waltz; the slur-staccato articulations will help you bring out this particular style.
Practise this slowly, in 3, and then gradually build up the speed until it feels like 1 count per bar.

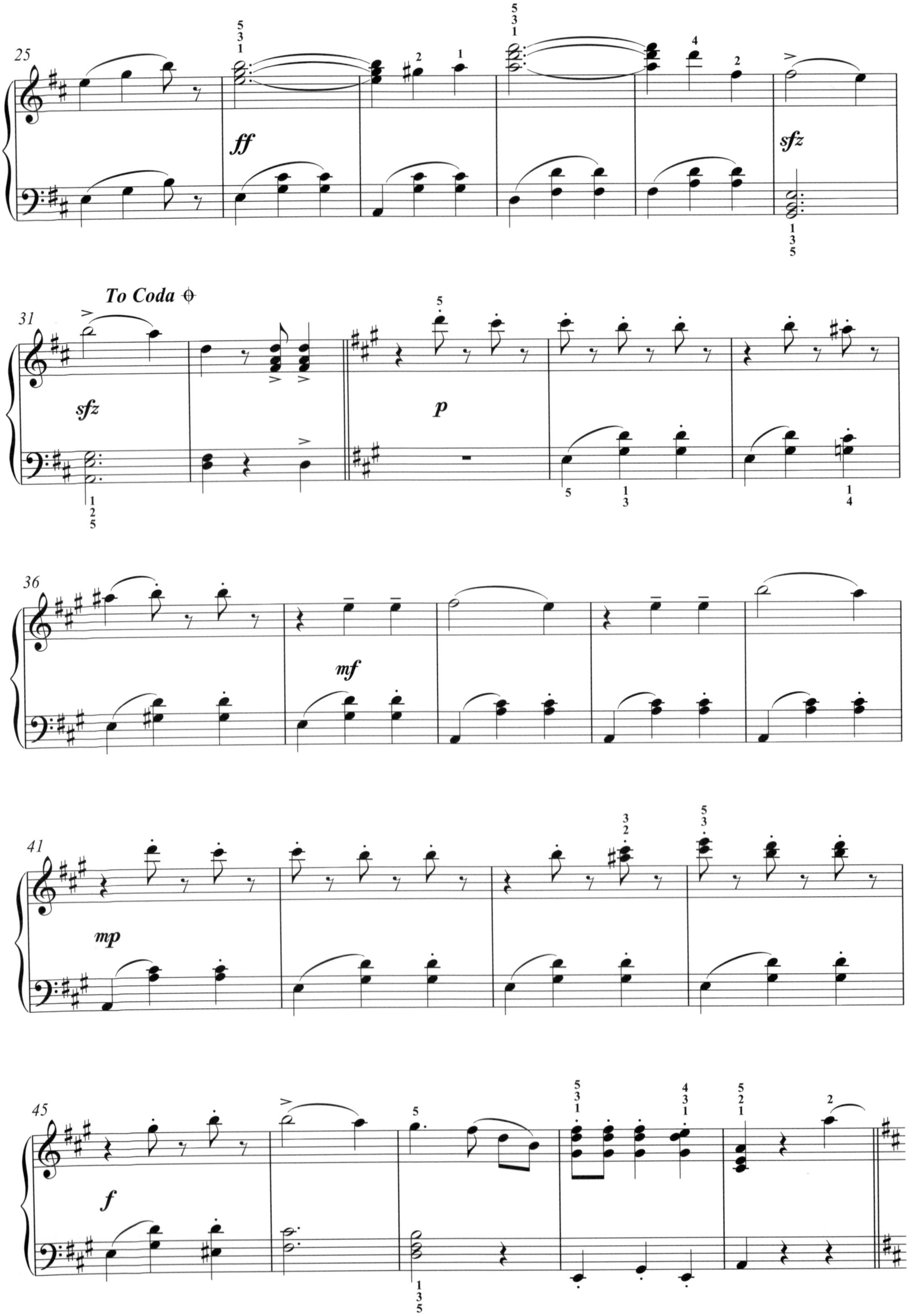
To Coda
ff
sfz
p
mf
mp
f

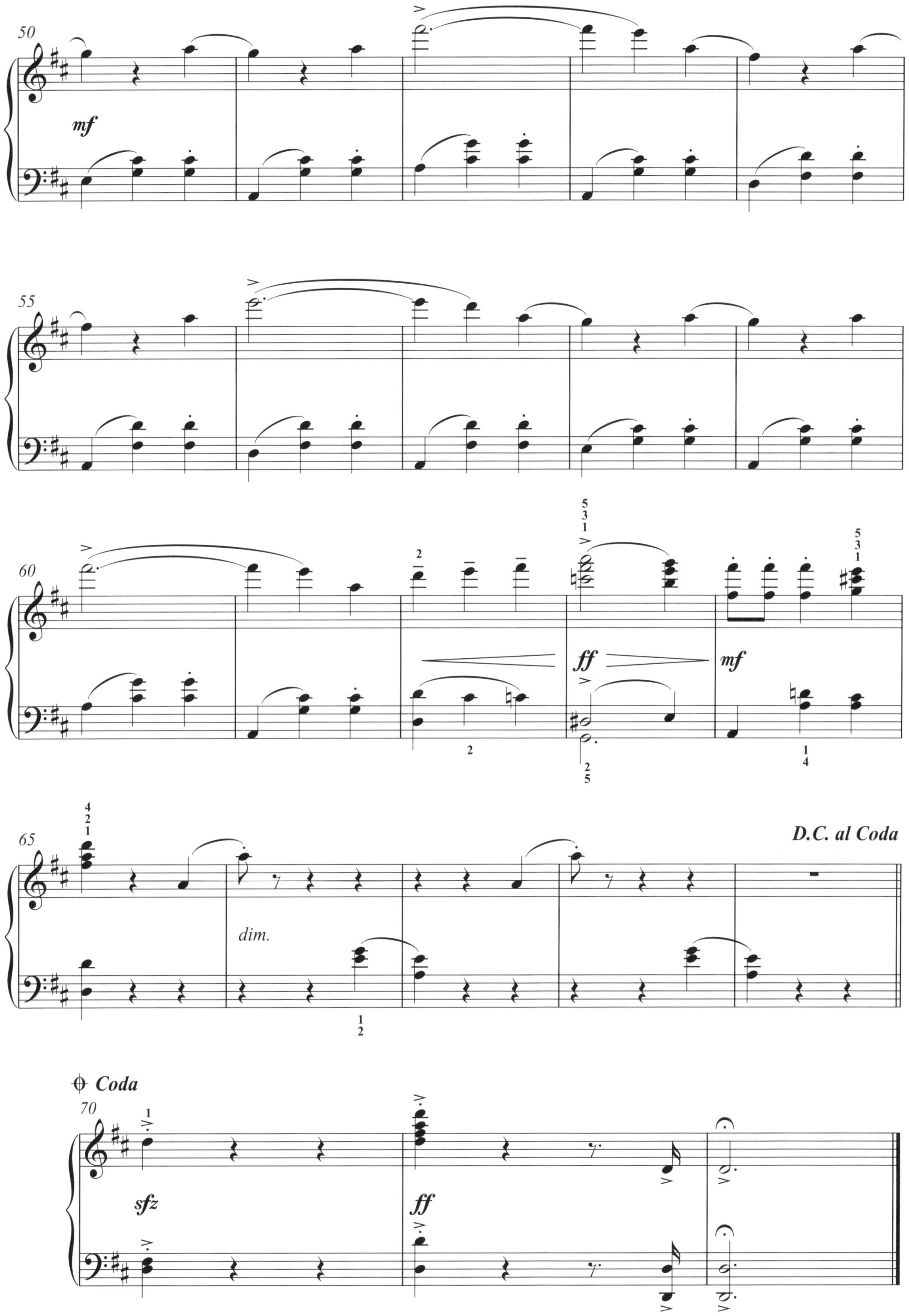
50
mf
55
60
ff
mf
65
D.C. al Coda
dim.
Coda
70
sfz
ff

En Bateau

Music by Claude Debussy

This piece was originally written as a piano duet.
However, it might be worth listening to the orchestral arrangement as you should to try and imitate an orchestral sound.
The two-against-three rhythm is tricky; keep the dotted crotchet pulse in your mind.

9

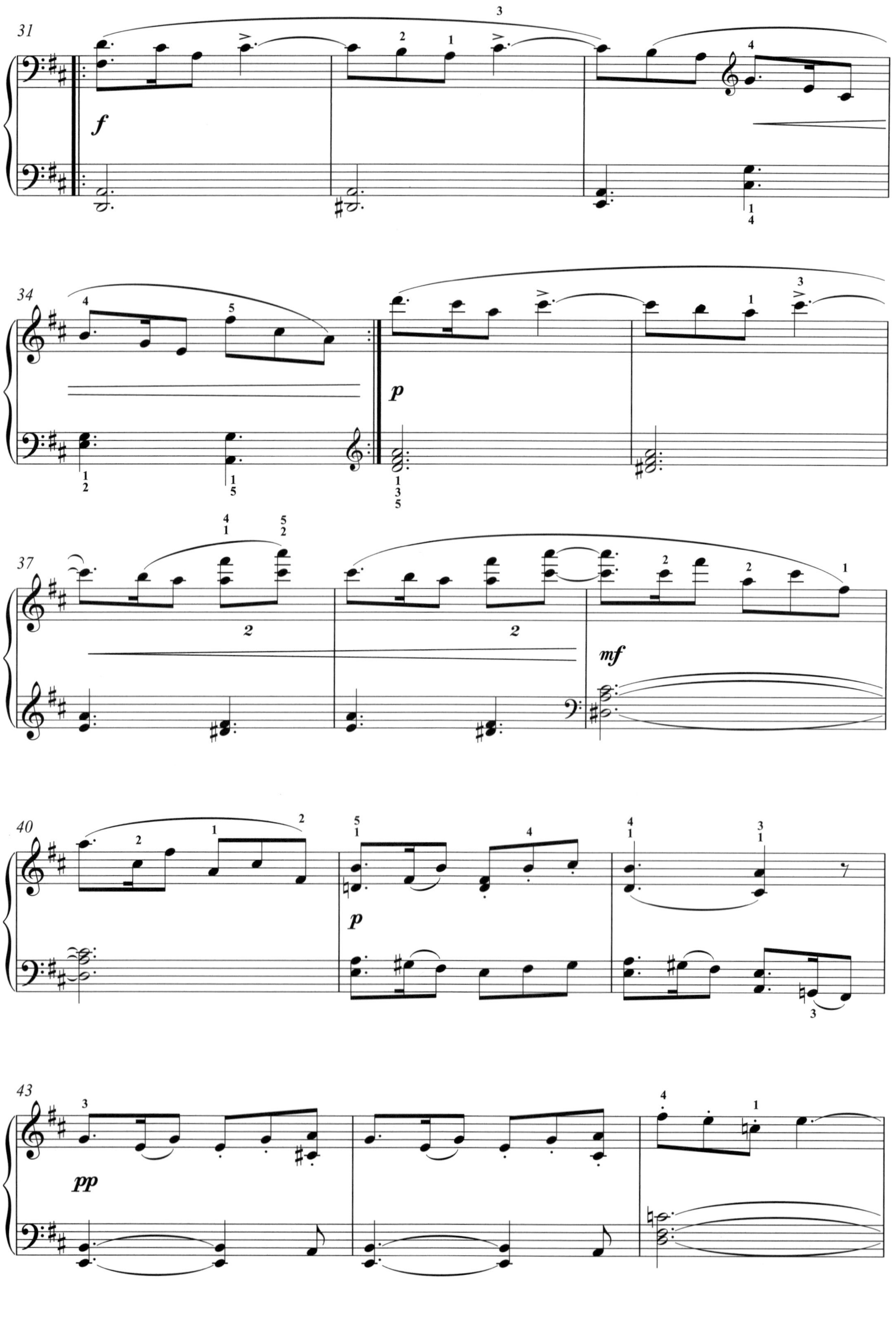
31
f
34
p
37
mf
40
p
43
pp

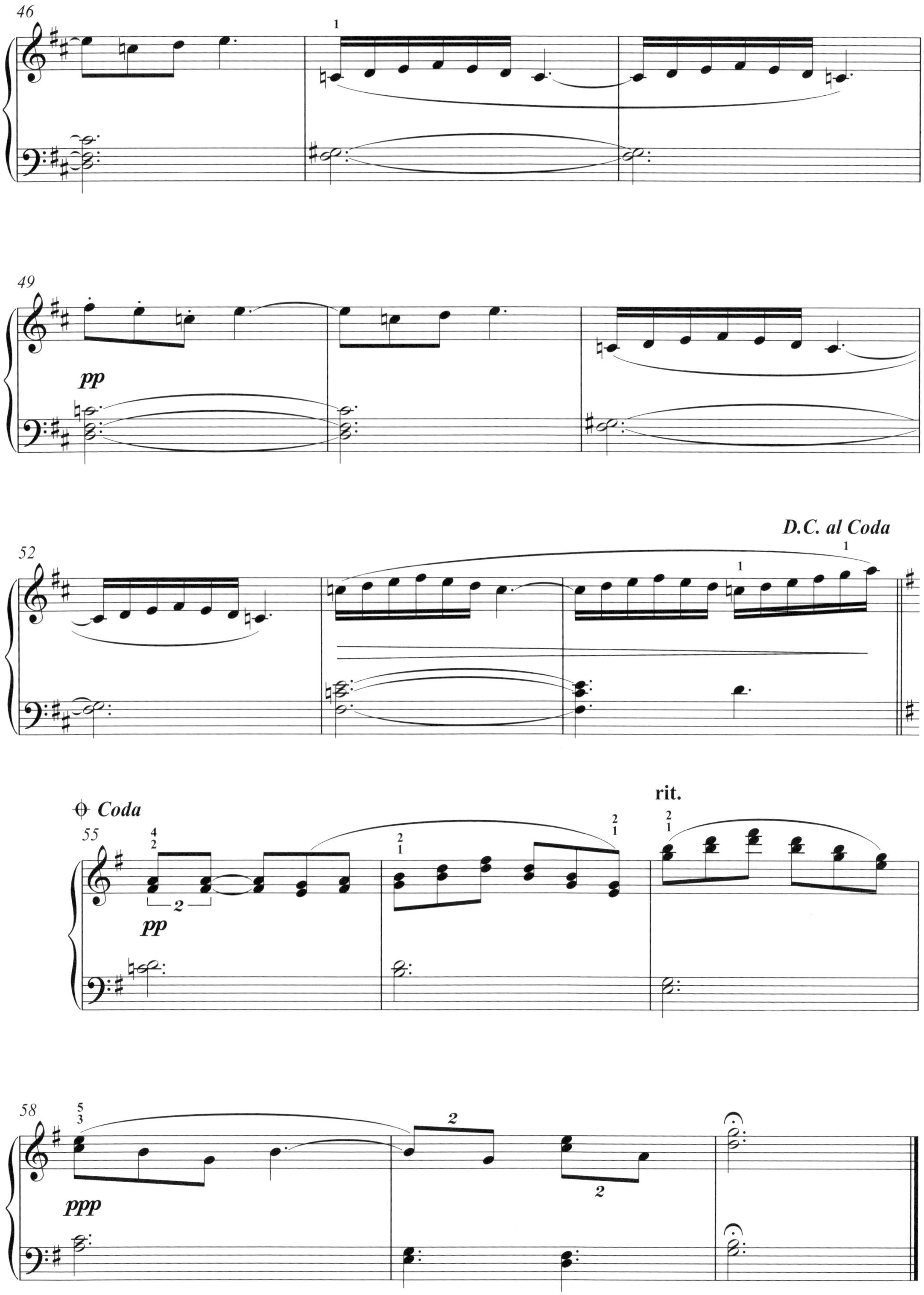
pp
D.C. al Coda
Coda
pp
rit.
ppp

Erla's Waltz

Music by Ólafur Arnalds

Try to keep the left hand soft so that you can clearly bring out the melody line above.
When pedalling, make sure you lift the pedal every bar to avoid over-blurring the sound.

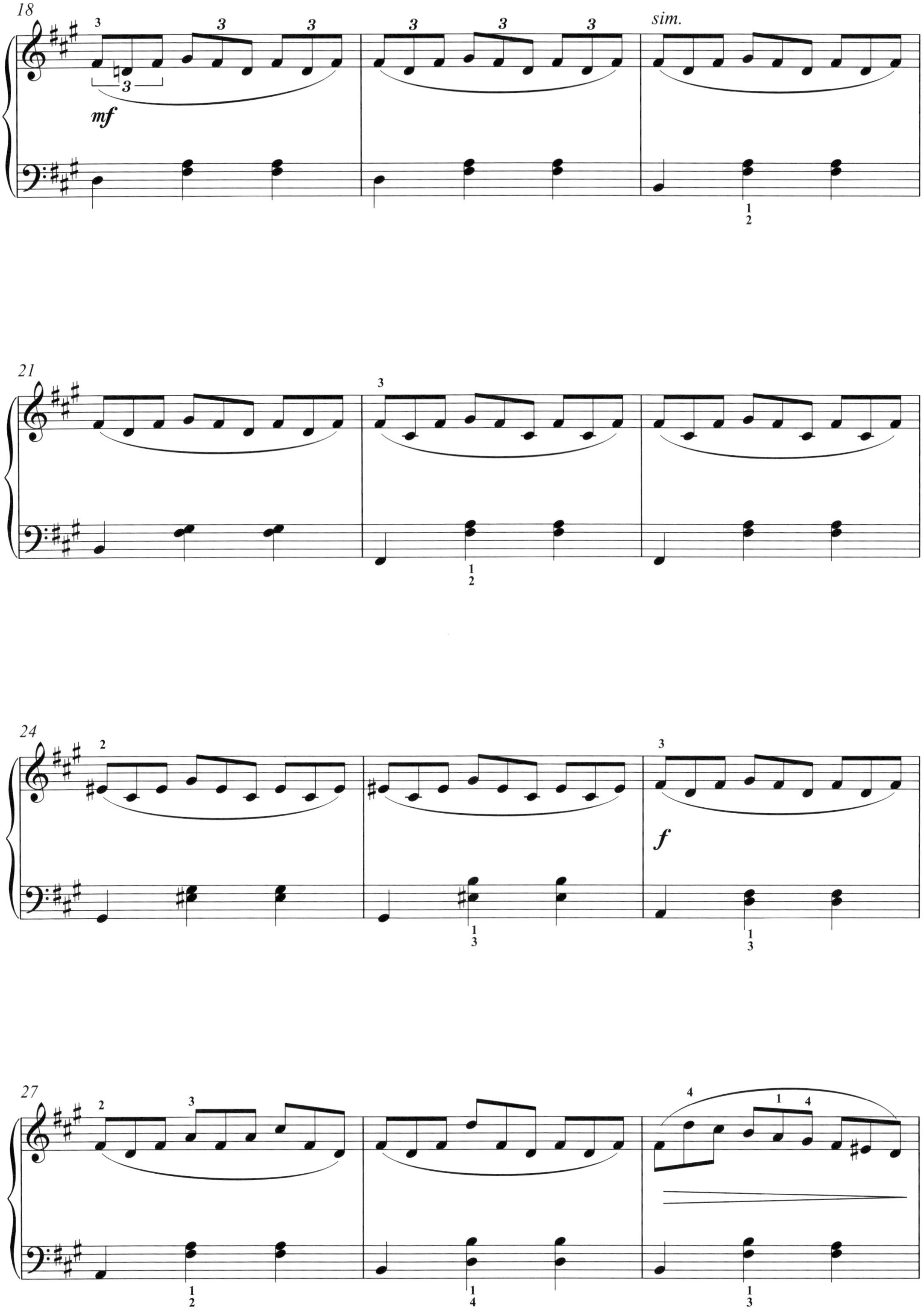
sim.

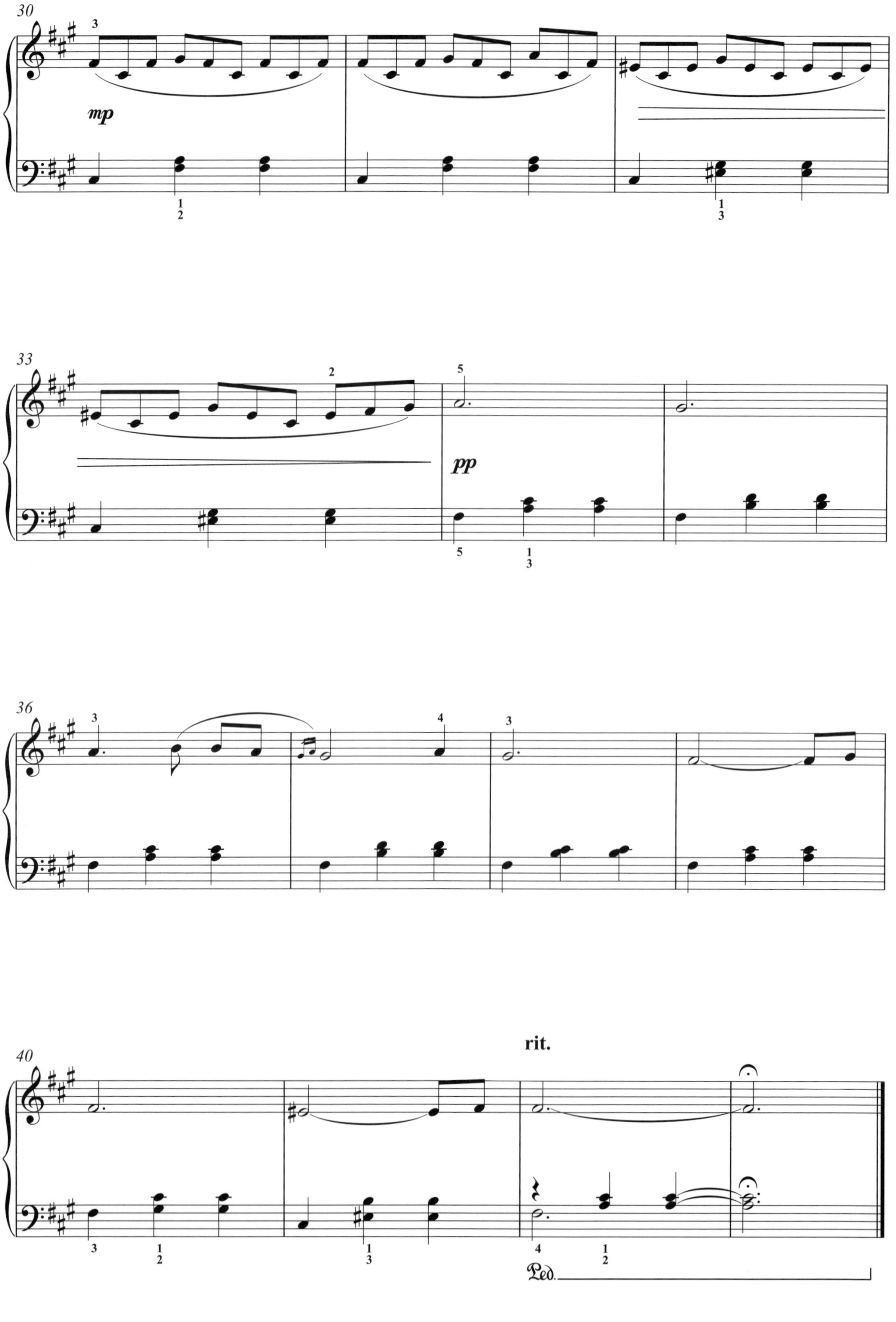
mp
pp
rit.
Ped.

The Family
(from *Lore*)

Music by Max Richter

This piece has a mood of stillness; think carefully about the atmosphere you might create from this with your playing. Increases and decreases in dynamic should be followed calmly and precisely.

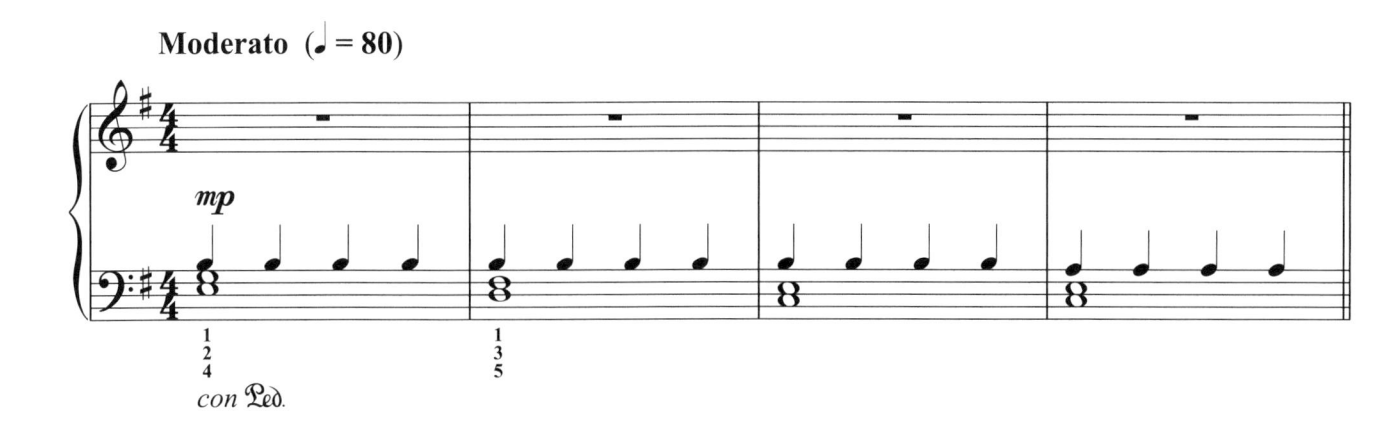

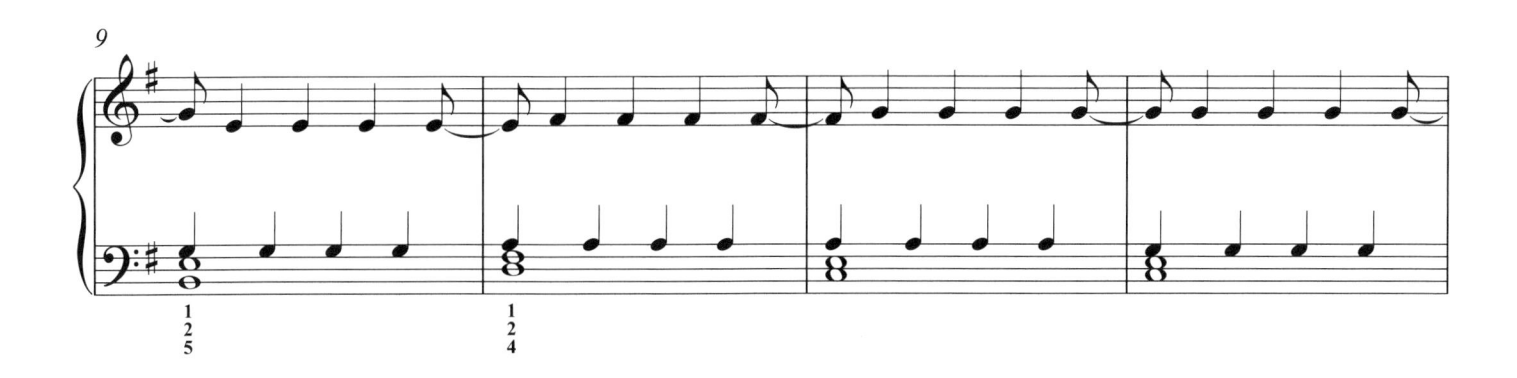

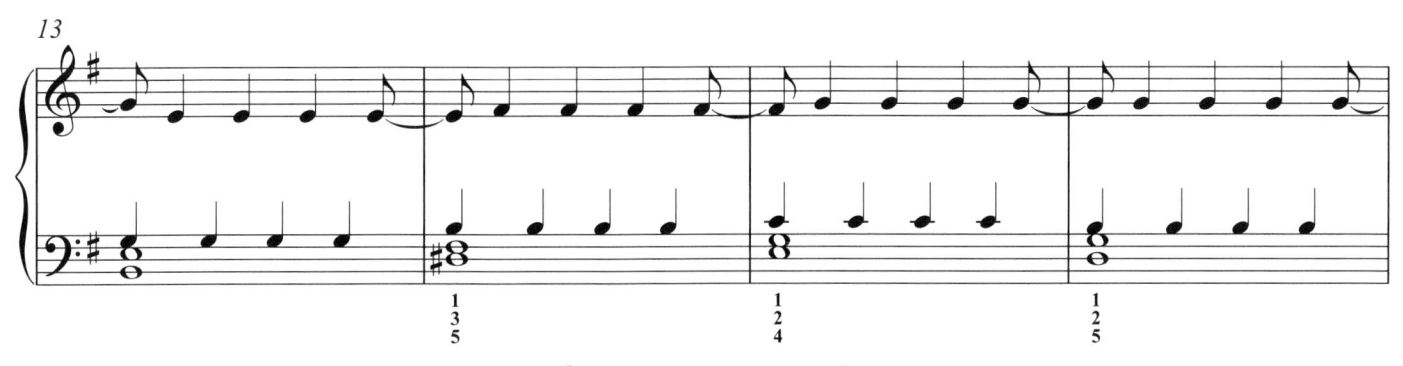

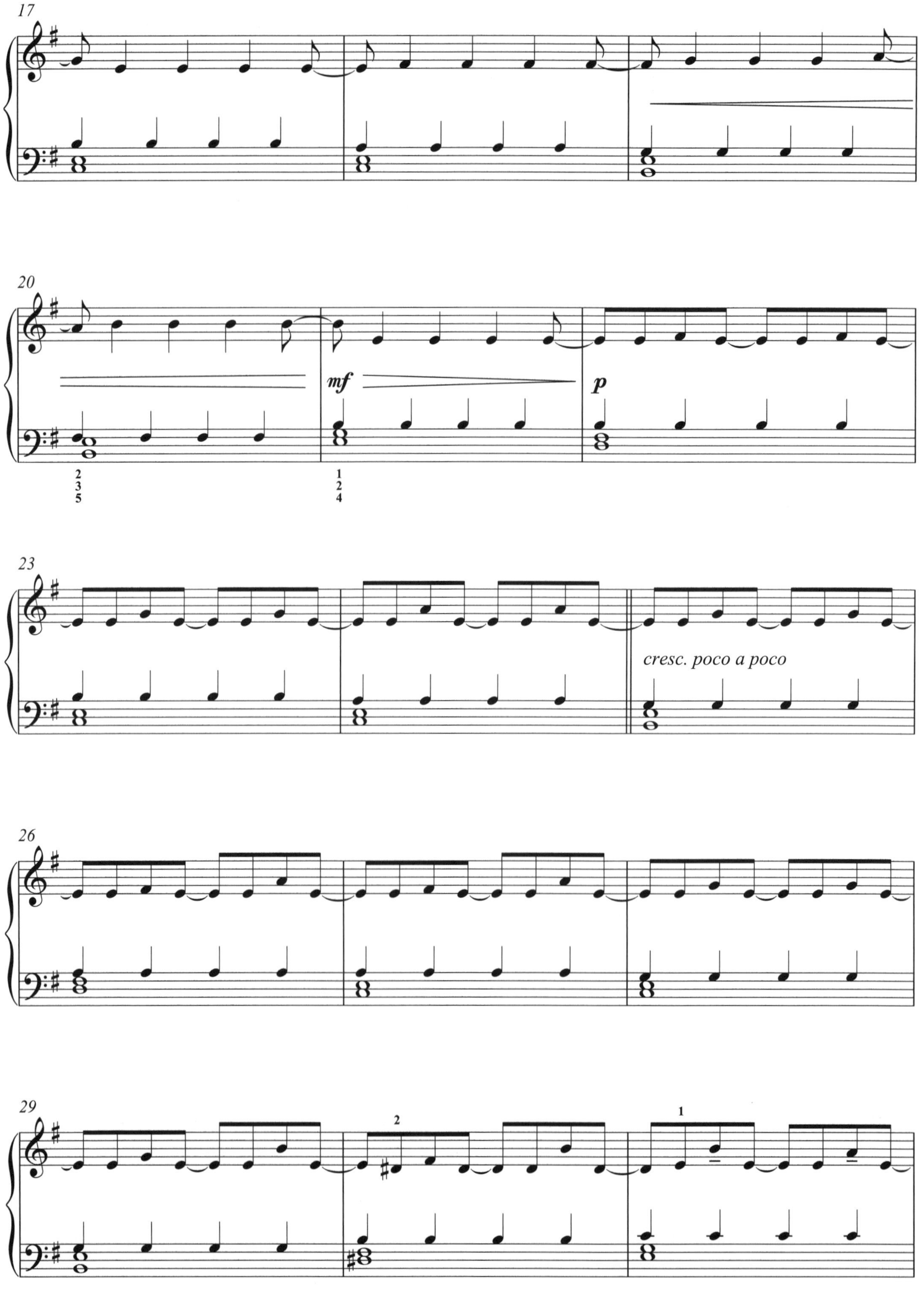
17
20
mf
p
2 3 5
1 2 4
23
cresc. poco a poco
26
29
2
1

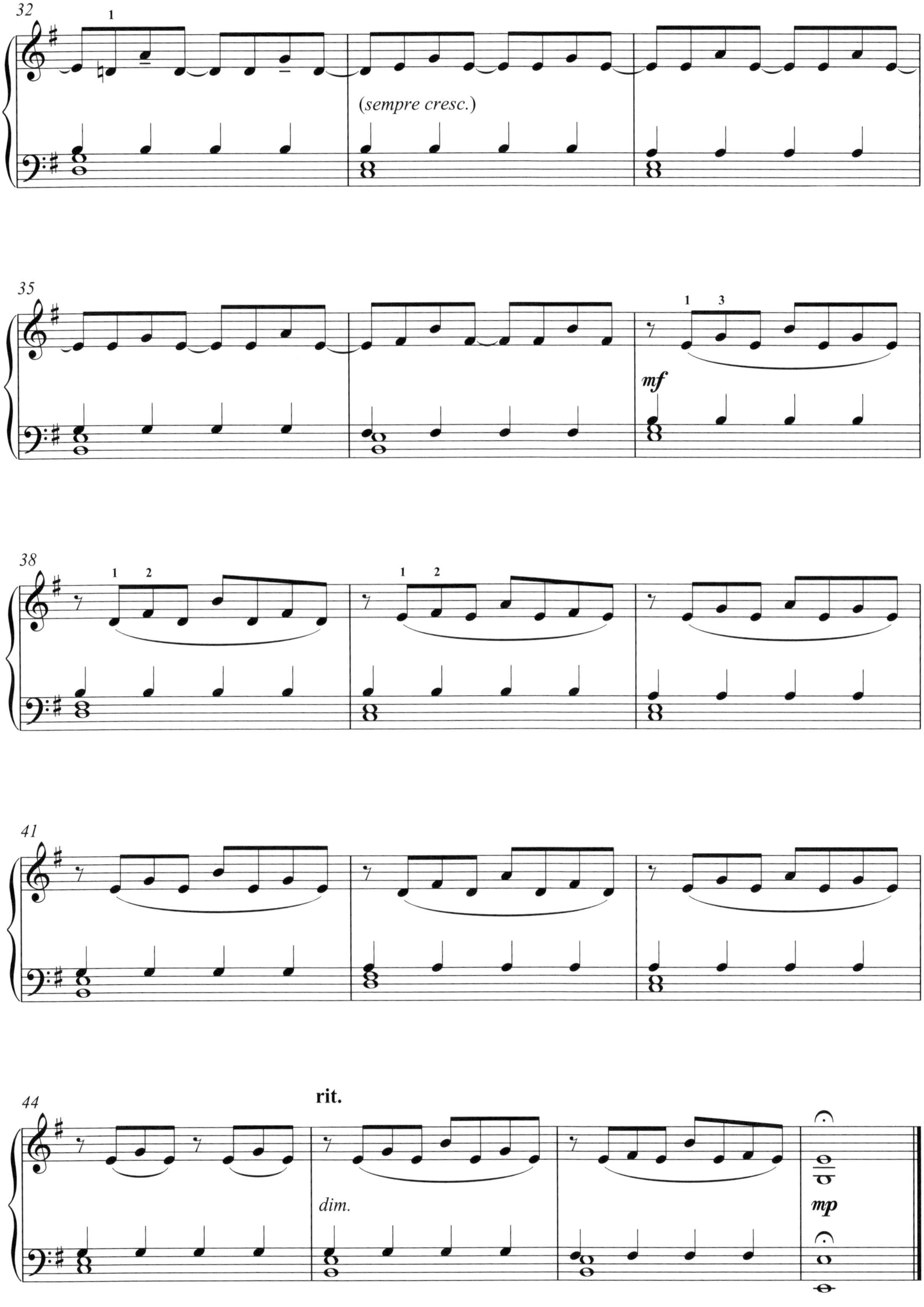
32
(sempre cresc.)
35
mf
38
41
44
rit.
dim.
mp

The Girl From Ipanema

Words by Norman Gimbel & Vinicius De Moraes
Music by Antonio Carlos Jobim

This piece requires a real lightness of touch. Keep a steady '4' pulse in mind as you play the syncopated passages. The right hand should be very legato in the middle phrases.

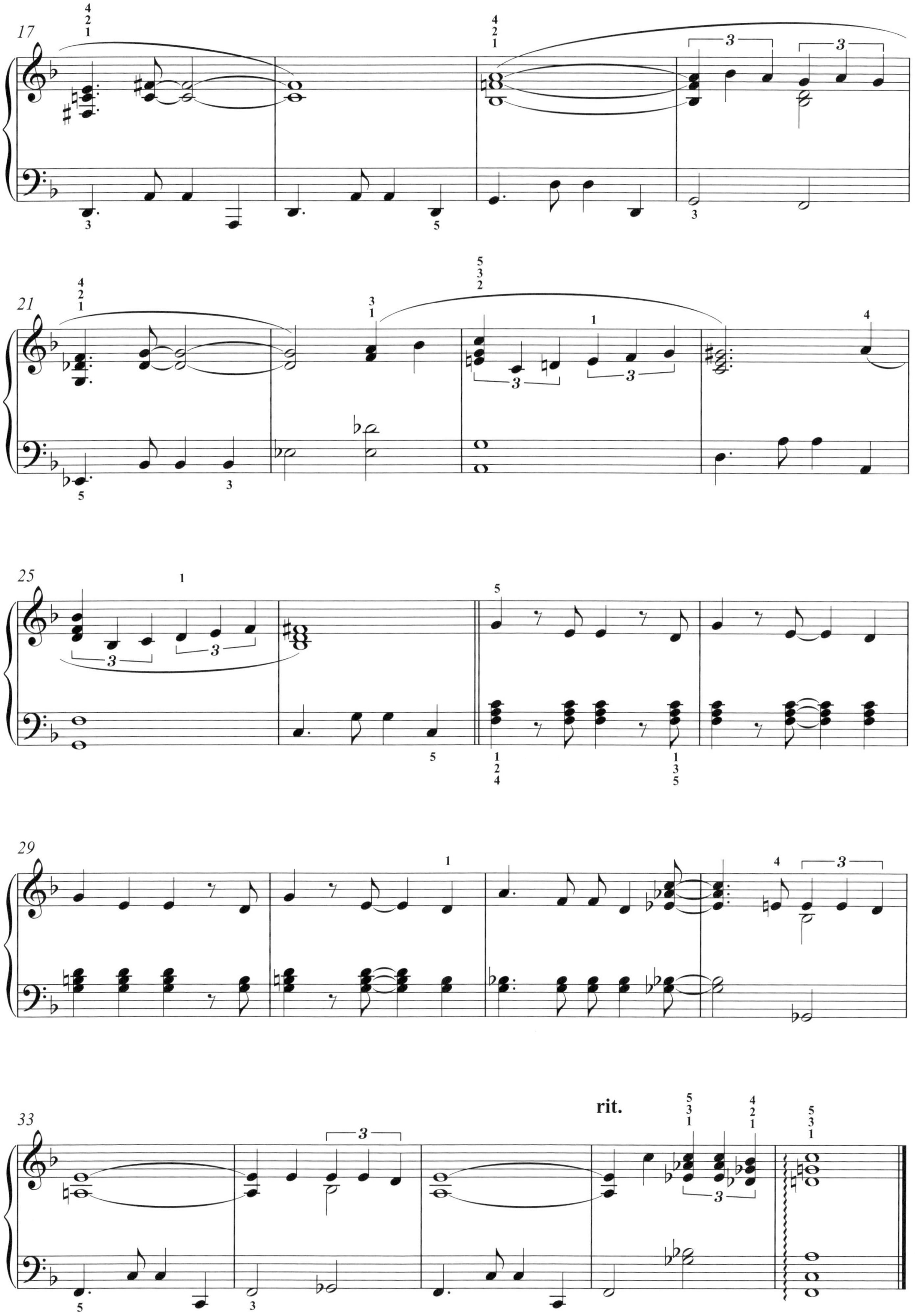

rit.

Habanera
(from Carmen)

Music by Georges Bizet
This is one of the most famous arias from the opera *Carmen*.
The left hand plays an ostinato inspired by the rhythm of the Spanish dance throughout most of the piece.
Watch out for the occasional changes between triplet and and dotted rhythms, making sure to play these with careful timing.

© Copyright 2017 Dorsey Brothers Music Limited.
All Rights Reserved. International Copyright Secured.

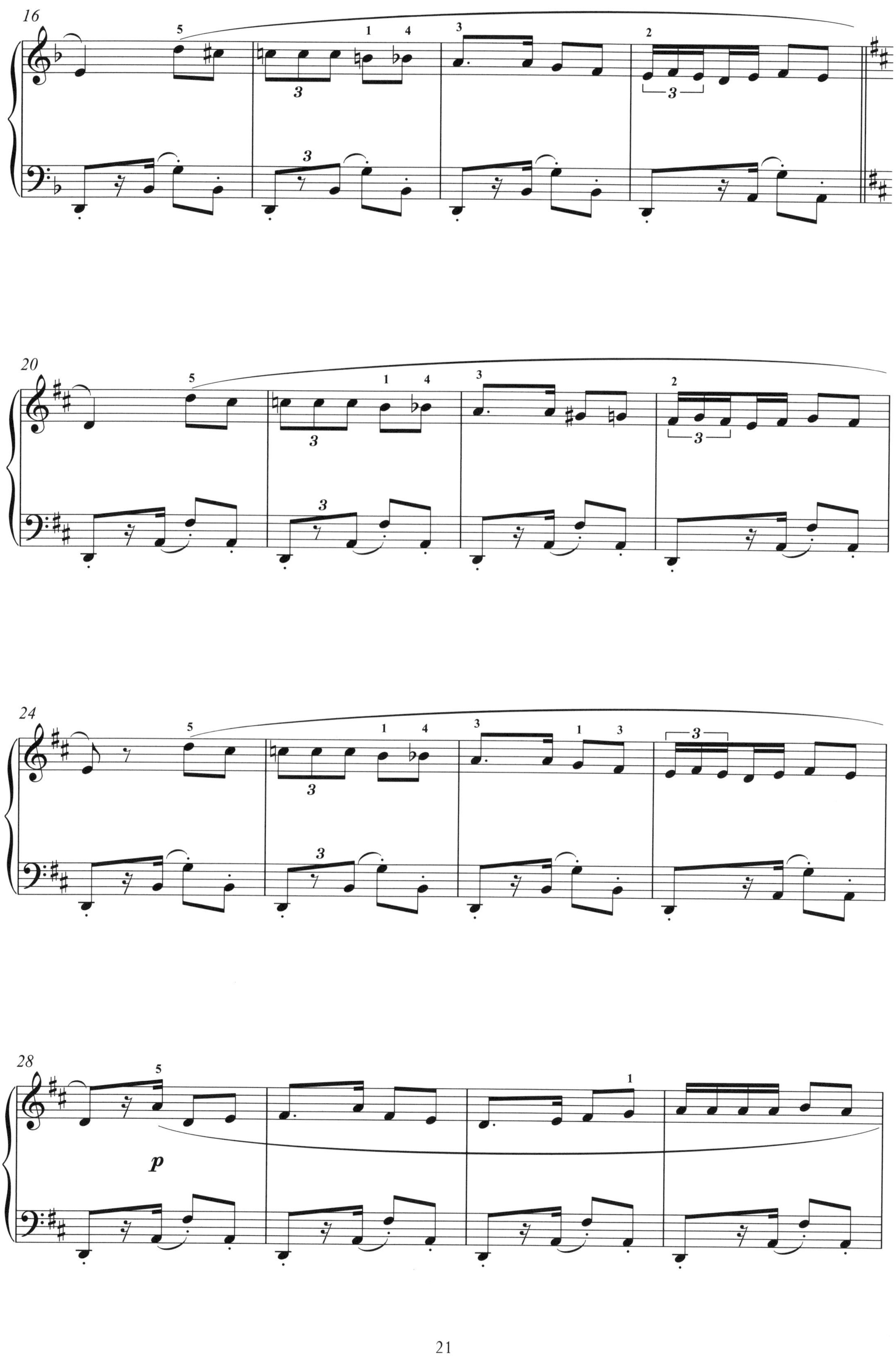
16
20
24
28
p

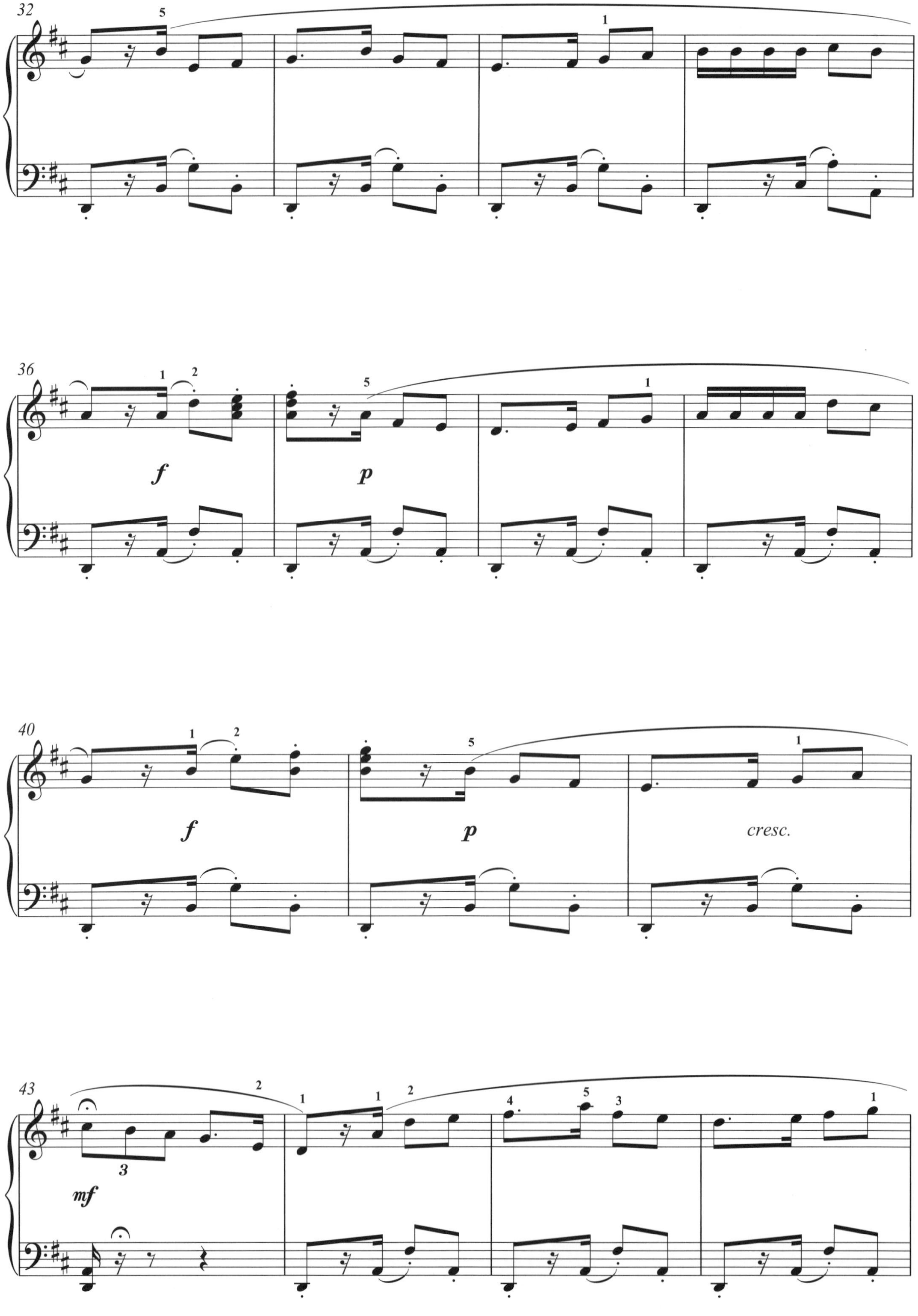
32
36
f
p
40
f
p
cresc.
43
mf

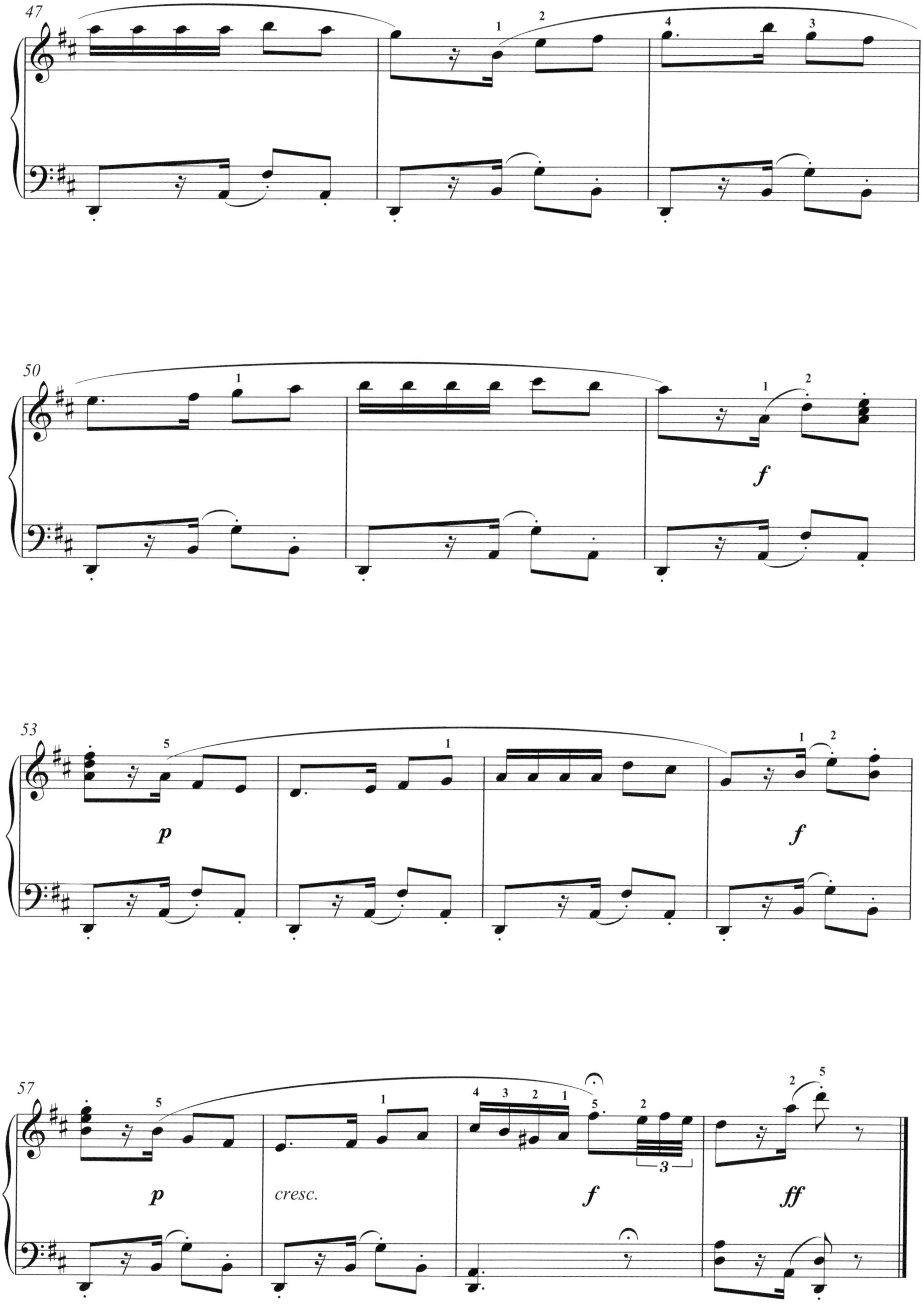
47
50
f
53
p
f
57
p
cresc.
f
ff

The James Bond Theme

Music by Monty Norman

This is the famous theme tune that appears in all of the James Bond movies. It needs plenty of separate hand practice; keep a relaxed wrist to play the repeated left-hand notes. Note how the rhythm changes at bar 30: quavers are swung from here on. Try to evoke the sound of Big Band Jazz.

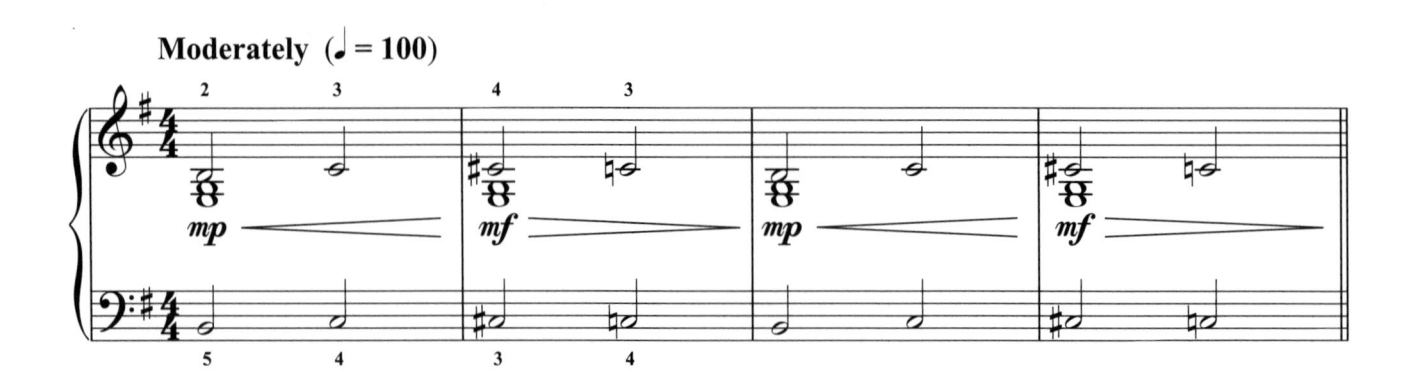

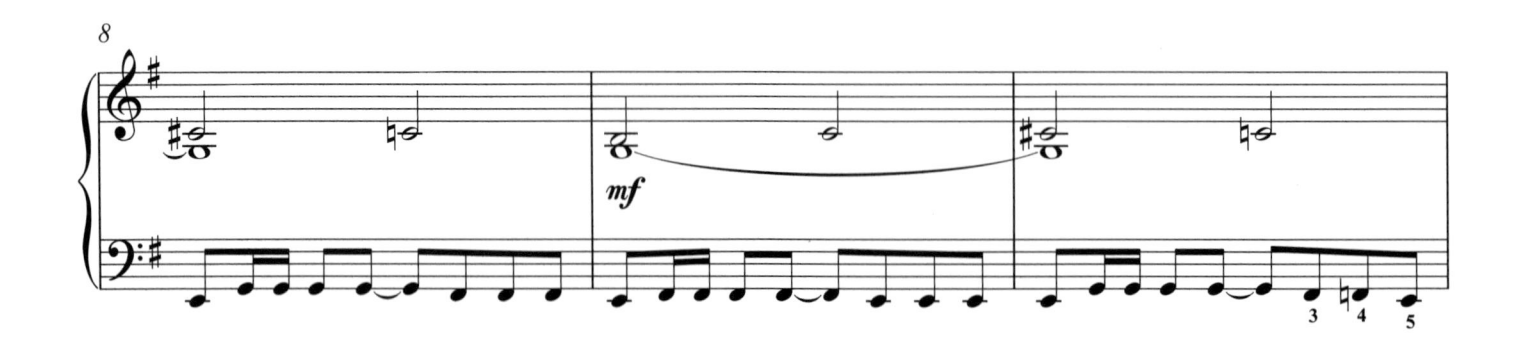

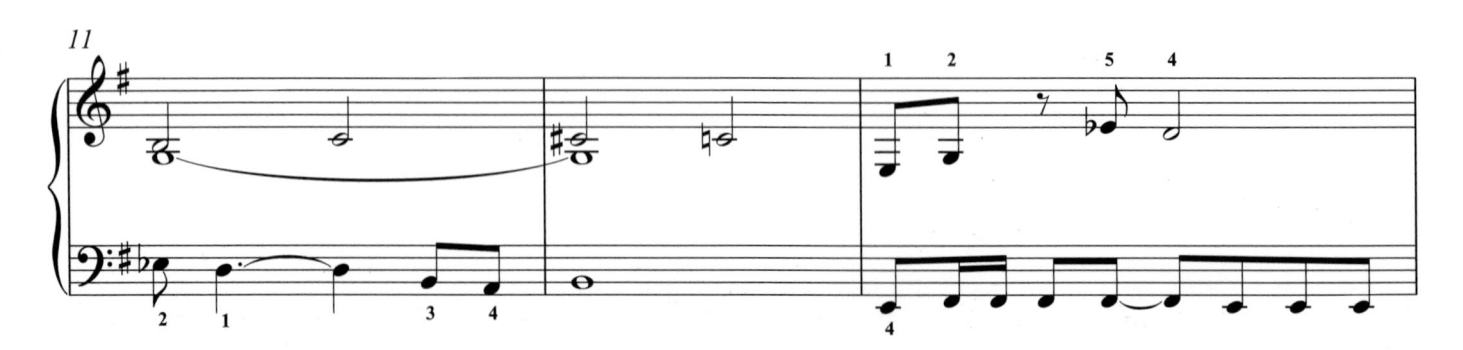

© Copyright 1962 EMI United Partnership Limited.
All Rights Reserved. International Copyright Secured.

25

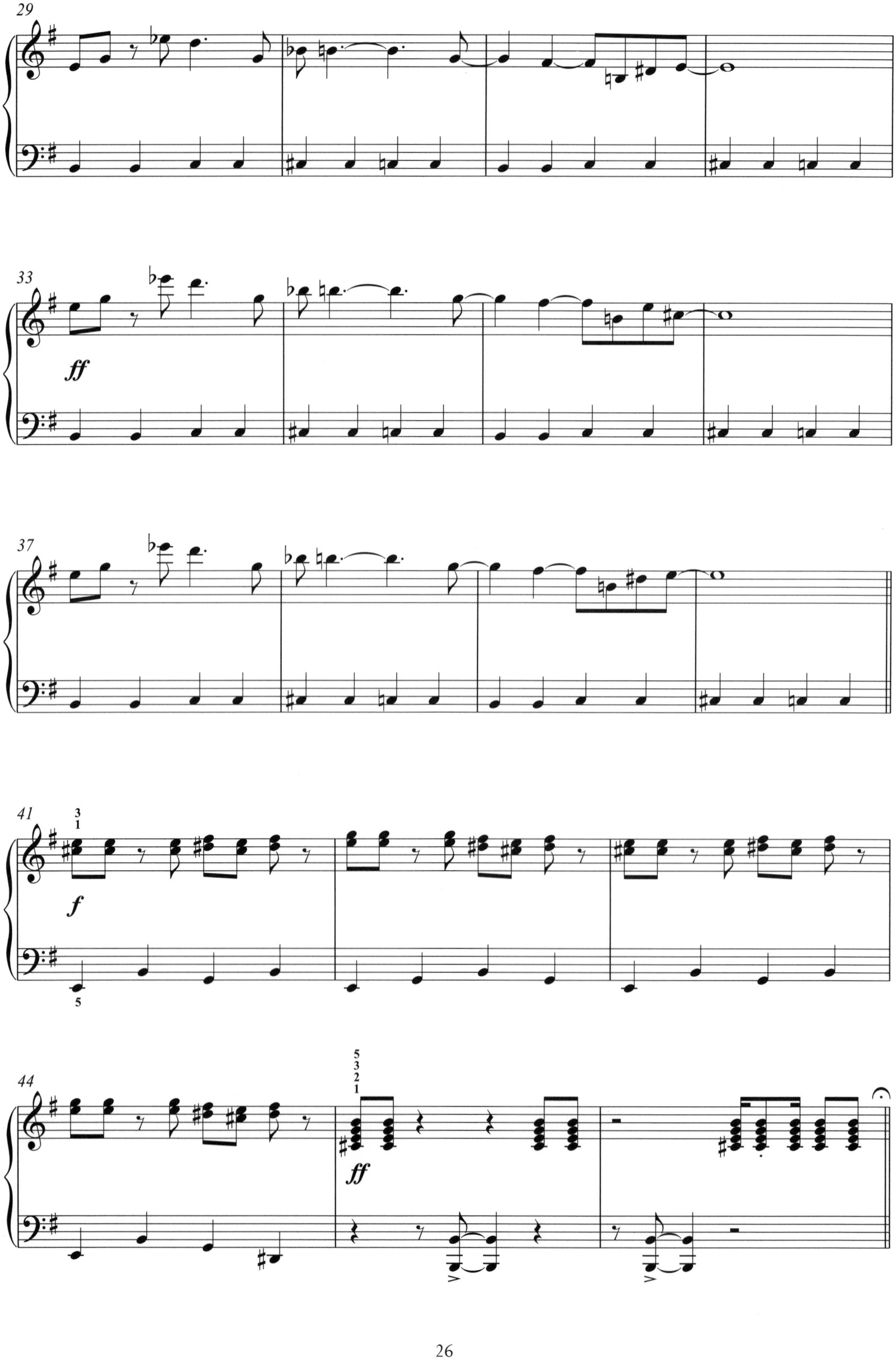
29
33
ff
37
41
f
44
ff

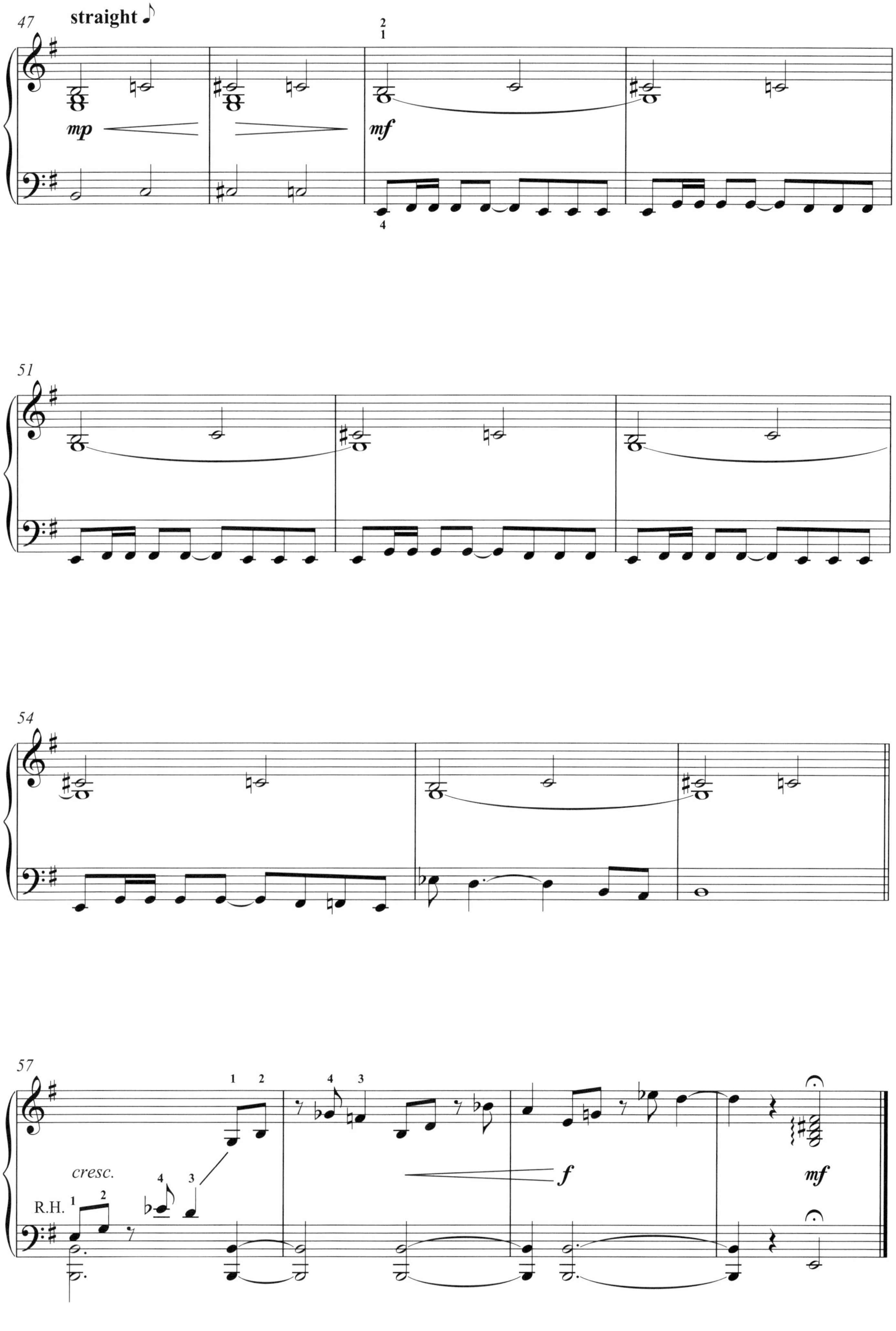
47
straight
mp
mf
51
54
57
cresc.
R.H.
f
mf

Larghetto
(No. 4 from *Les Cinq Doigts*)

Music by Igor Stravinsky

The 6/8 metre and the gentle dotted rhythms in the right hand give this piece a lilting quality.
The beginning should be soft and gentle, but the second half needs a louder dynamic.

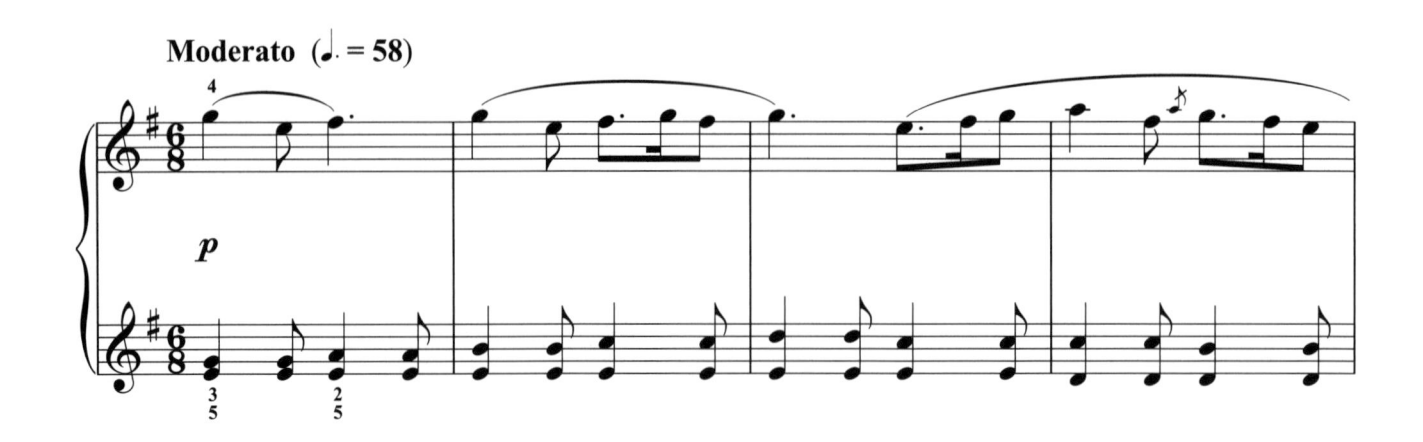

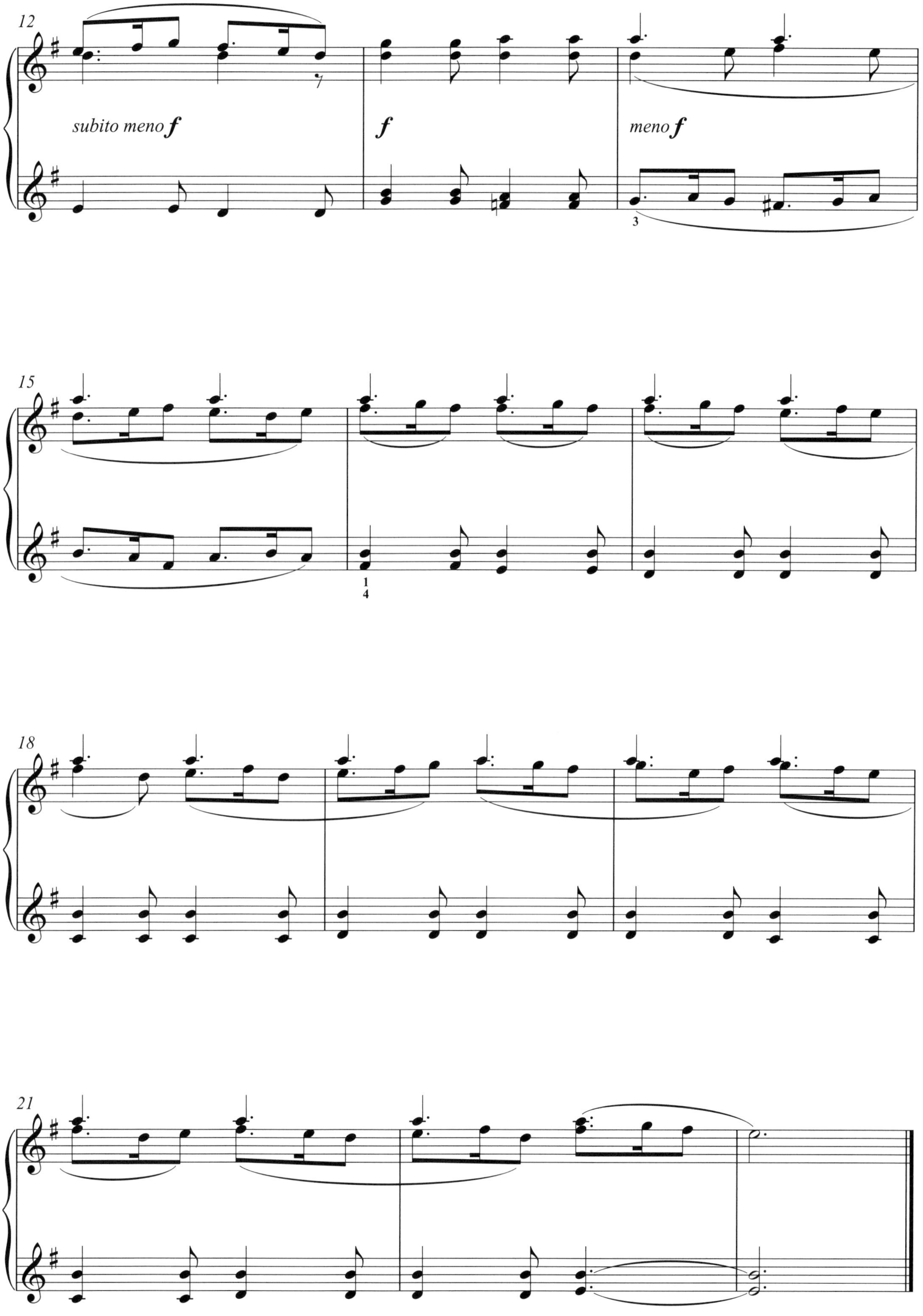
12
subito meno f
f
meno f
3
15
1
4
18
21

Lost!

Words & Music by Guy Berryman, Chris Martin, Jon Buckland & Will Champion

Most of this song is built upon the repetition of the same four chords. Enjoy the subtle changes when they come.
Try to emphasise the top notes in the right-hand chords, as these are part of the melody line.

© Copyright 2008 Universal Music Publishing MGB Limited.
All Rights Reserved. International Copyright Secured.

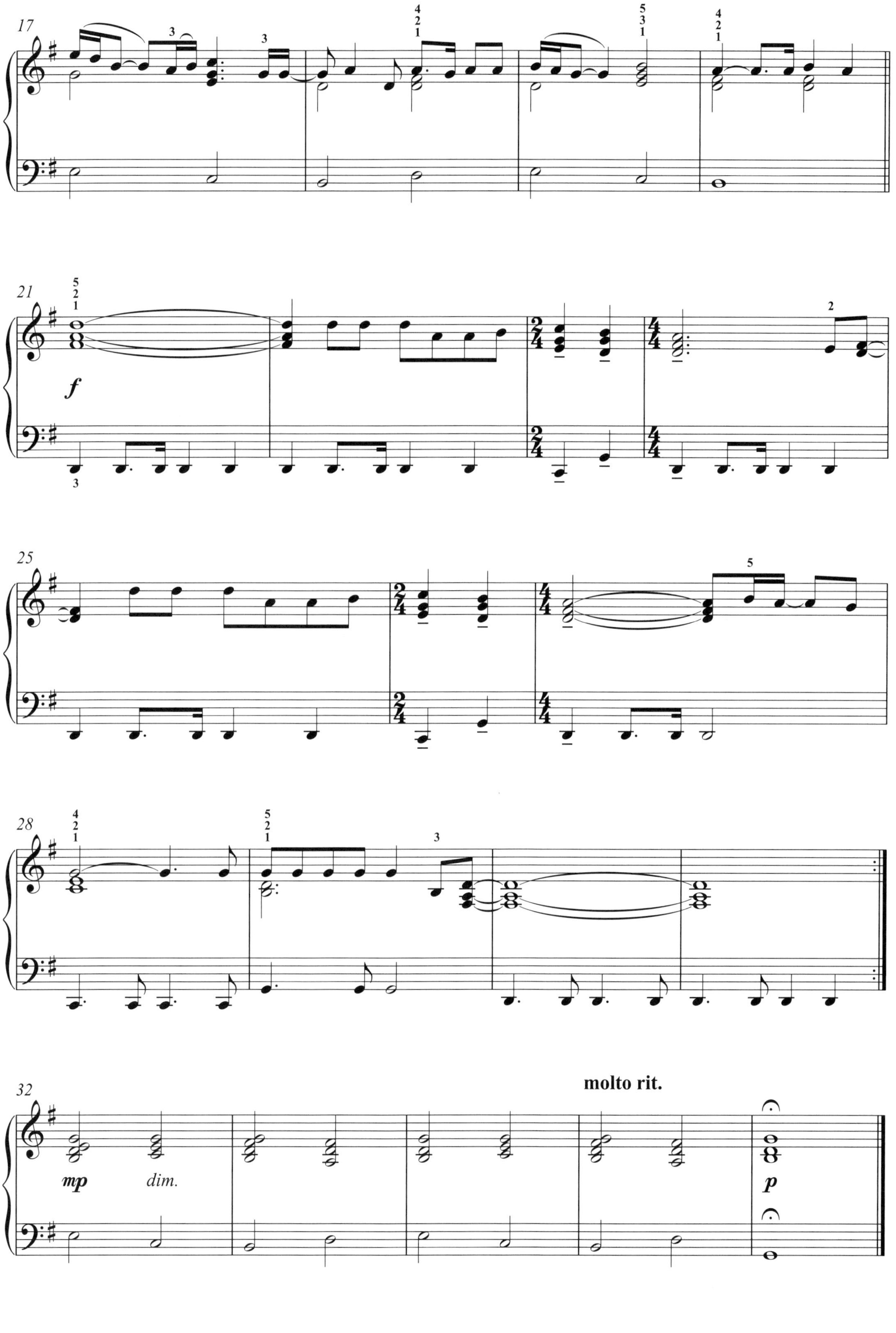
17
21
f
25
28
32
mp
dim.
molto rit.
p

Over The Rainbow

Words by E. Y. Harburg
Music by Harold Arlen

Enjoy the harmonies in this arrangement; listen carefully to the chromatic changes.
Notice all the tempo directions: the music needs to ebb and flow.

© Copyright 1939 EMI Feist Catalog Incorporated.
EMI United Partnership Limited.
All Rights Reserved. International Copyright Secured.

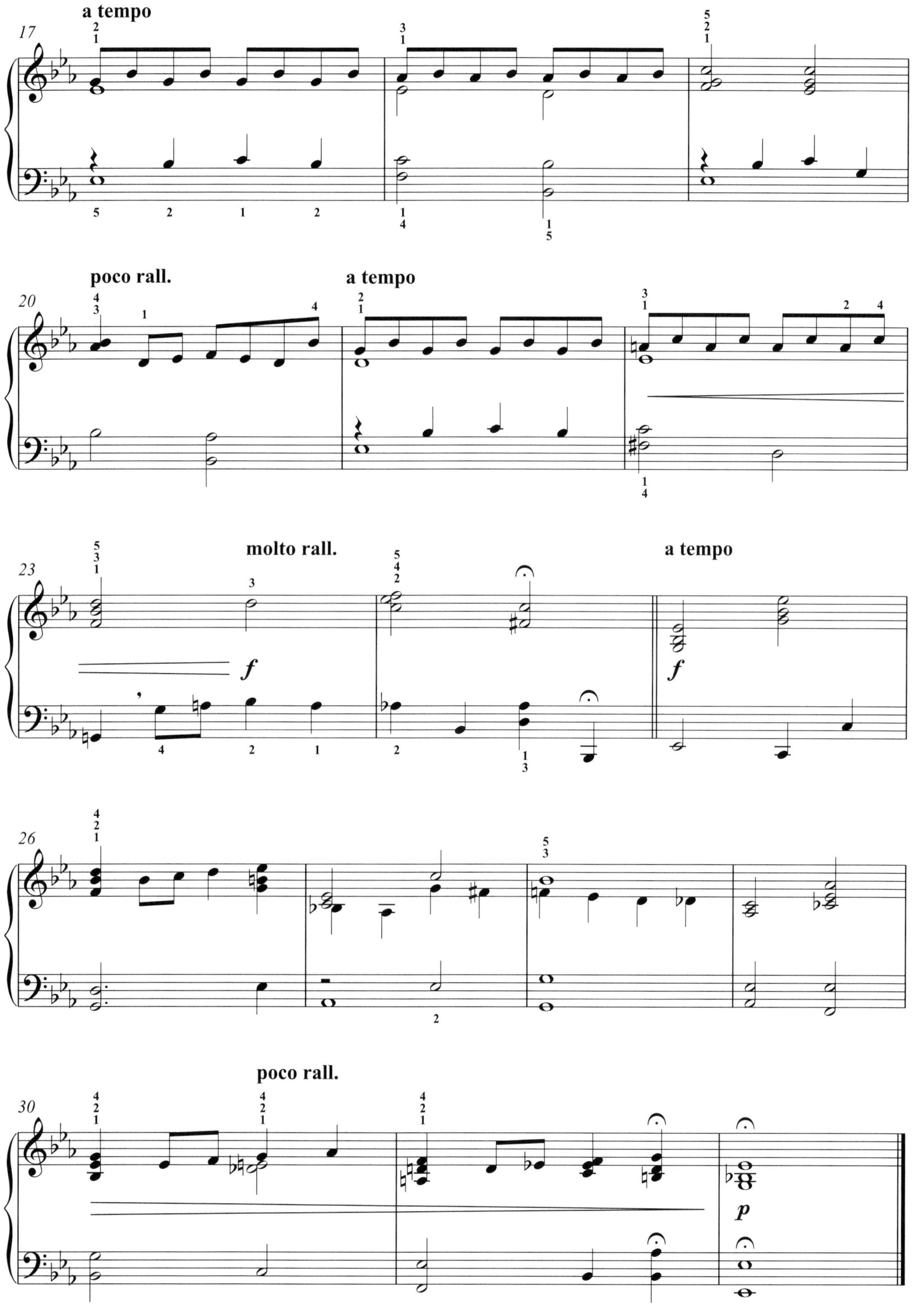
a tempo
poco rall.
a tempo
molto rall.
f
a tempo
f
poco rall.
p

Rolling In the Deep

Words & Music by Paul Epworth & Adele Adkins

Practise the left hand first so that you're confident with the driving beat.
You will need a strong sense of pulse to be able to play some of the tricky right-hand rhythms.

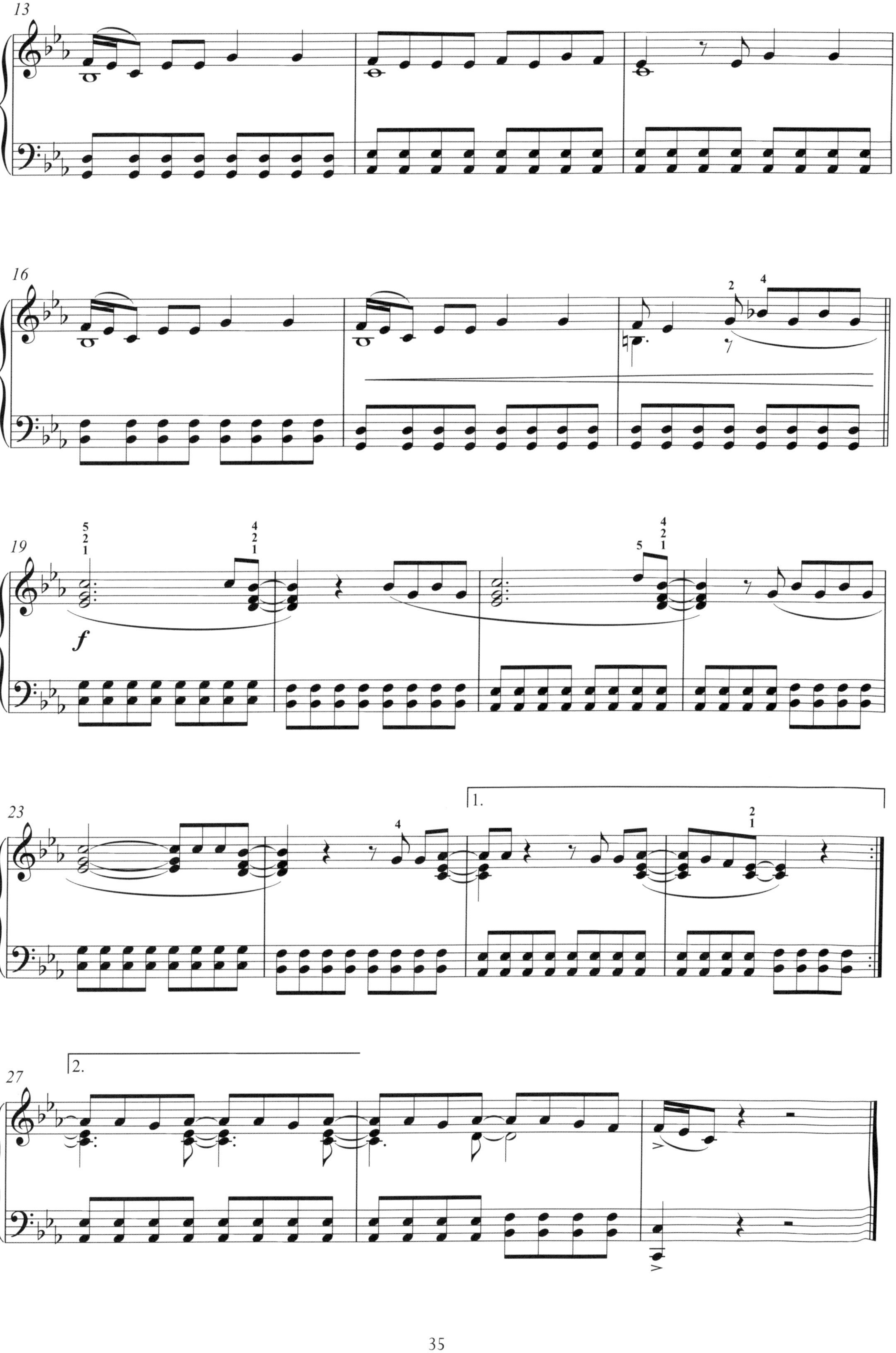
1.
2.

Somewhere Only We Know

Words & Music by Richard Hughes, Tim Rice-Oxley & Tom Chaplin

The left hand has a lot of work to do in this song. Separate hand practice will help you to get the correct dynamic and to get used to the movement of the left hand between bass and treble clefs from bar 13 to the end.
Some pedal will certainly help.

© Copyright 2004 BMG Music Publishing Limited.
Universal Music Publishing MGB Limited.
All Rights Reserved. International Copyright Secured.

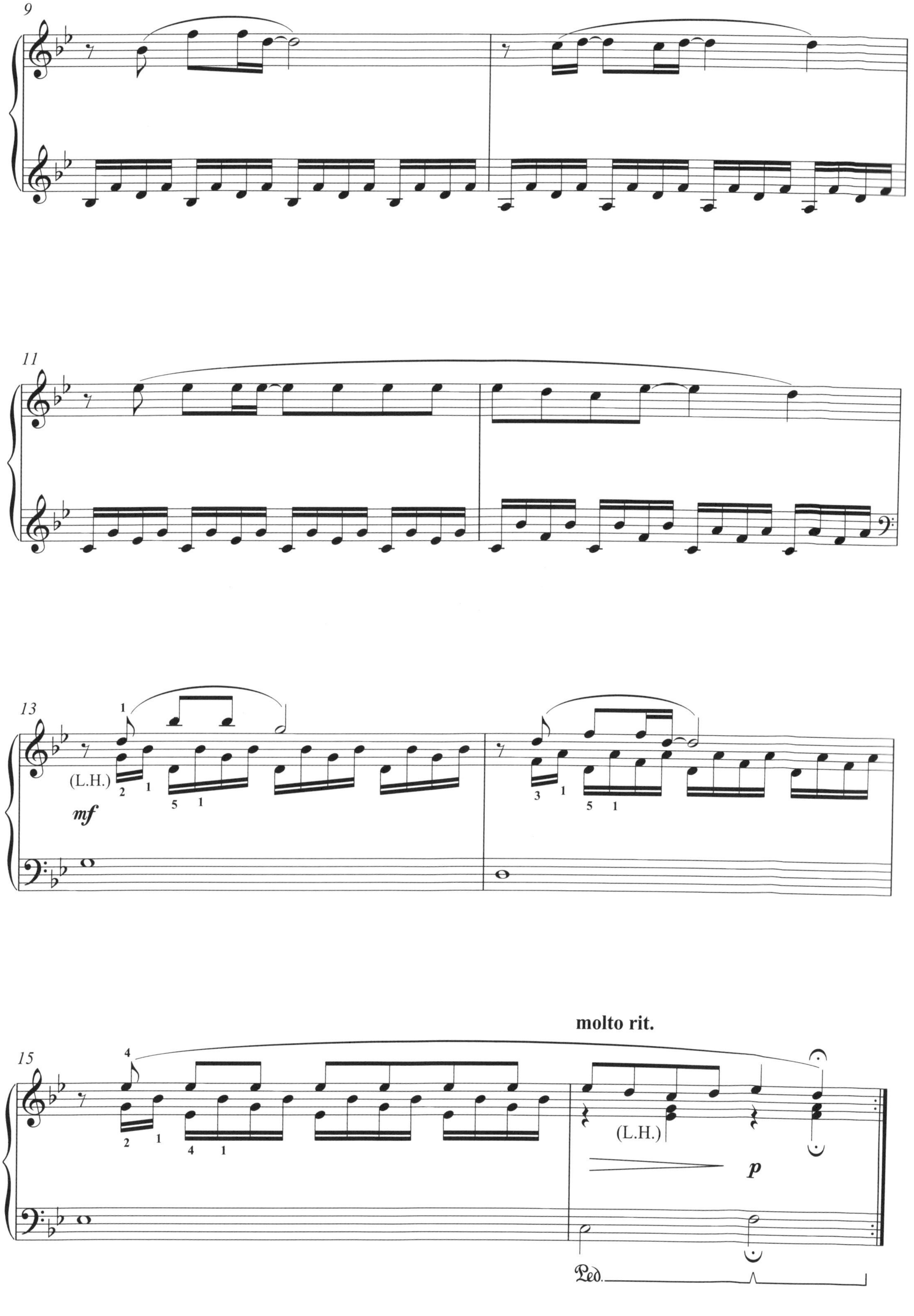
9
11
13
(L.H.)
mf
15
molto rit.
(L.H.)
p
Ped.

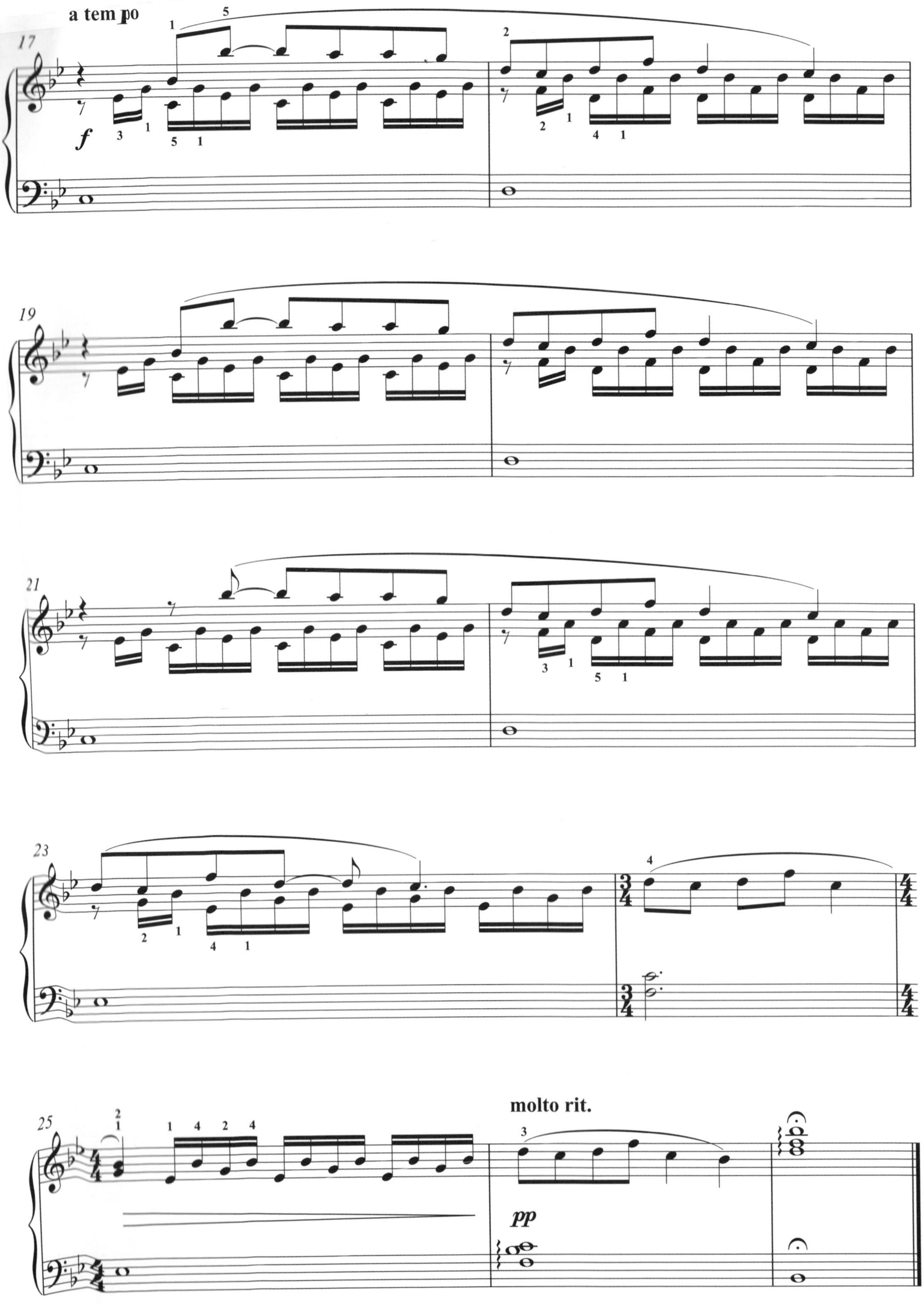
a tem po
f
molto rit.
pp

Song For Gavin

Music by Ludovico Einaudi

Keep the flowing right-hand semiquavers light and airy. Notice how the right hand actually plays more or less the same line throughout the piece. The changing harmonies in the left hand lend the piece an atmospheric subtlety; make sure to highlight these expressively. Remember that the tempo is rubato; take your time and immerse yourself in the mood.

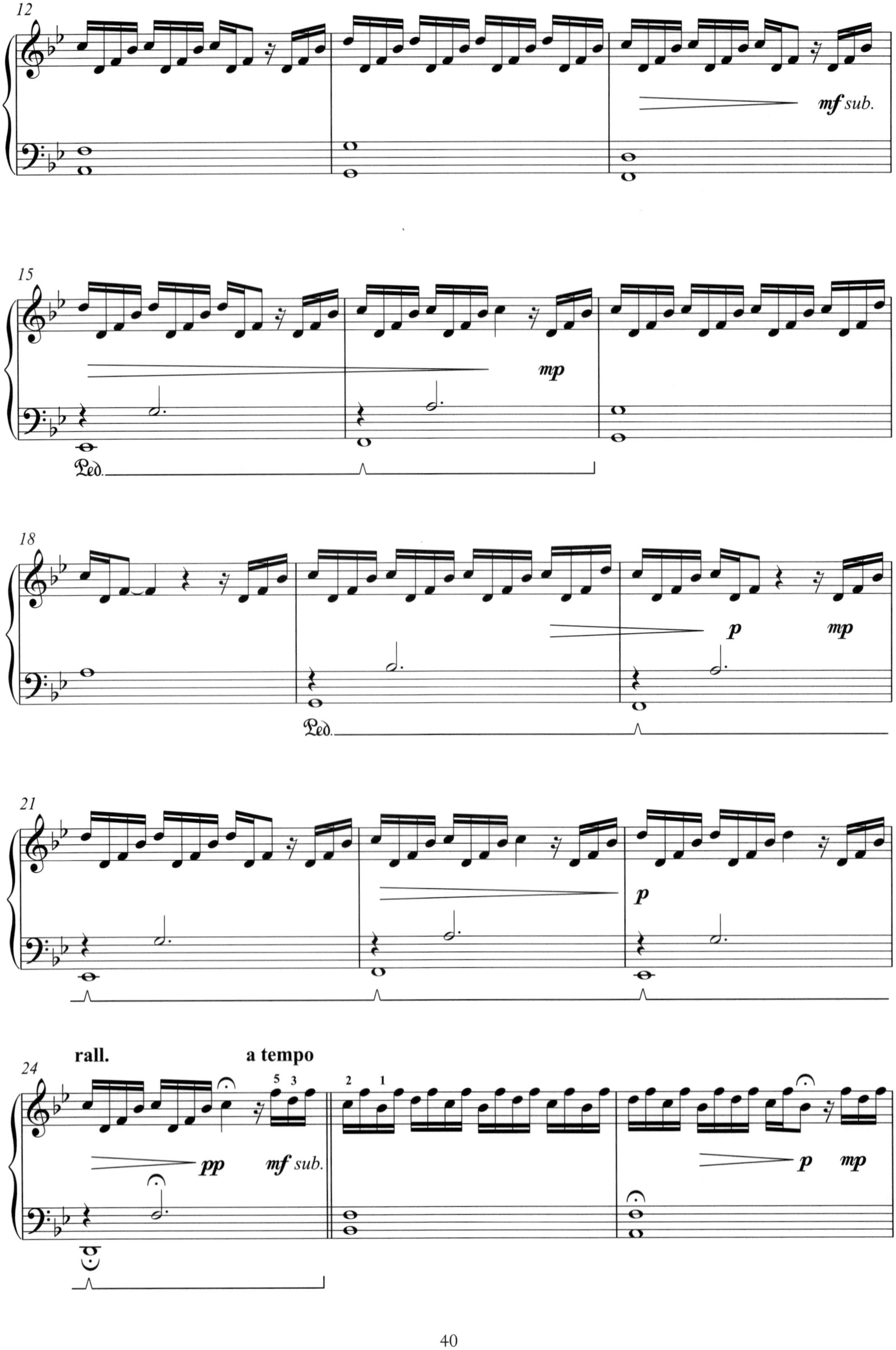
12
mf sub.
15
mp
Ped.
18
p
mp
Ped.
21
p
24
rall.
a tempo
pp
mf sub.
p
mp

41

Three Secrets From The Abyss: No. 1

Music by John Harle

This piece has a quiet simplicity. Dynamics are fairly even.
Let the reflective right-hand melody subtly soar above the sombre left-hand chords.

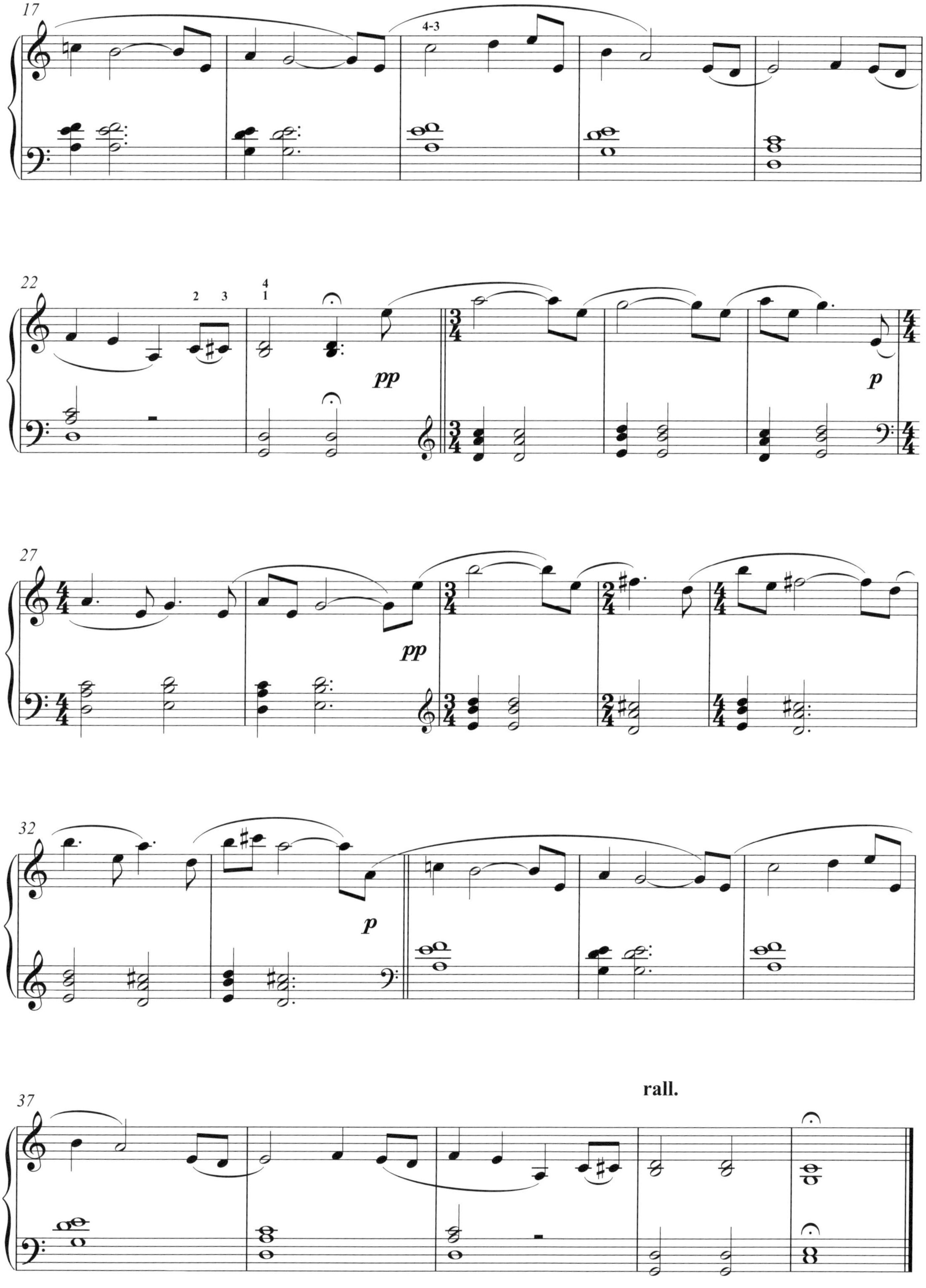
17
22
pp
p
27
pp
32
p
37
rall.

To A Wild Rose

Music by by Edward MacDowell

This is a charming little melody, from Macdowell's *10 Woodland Sketches, Op. 51*.
It should be simple and sweet, building to a climax around bars 25–28.

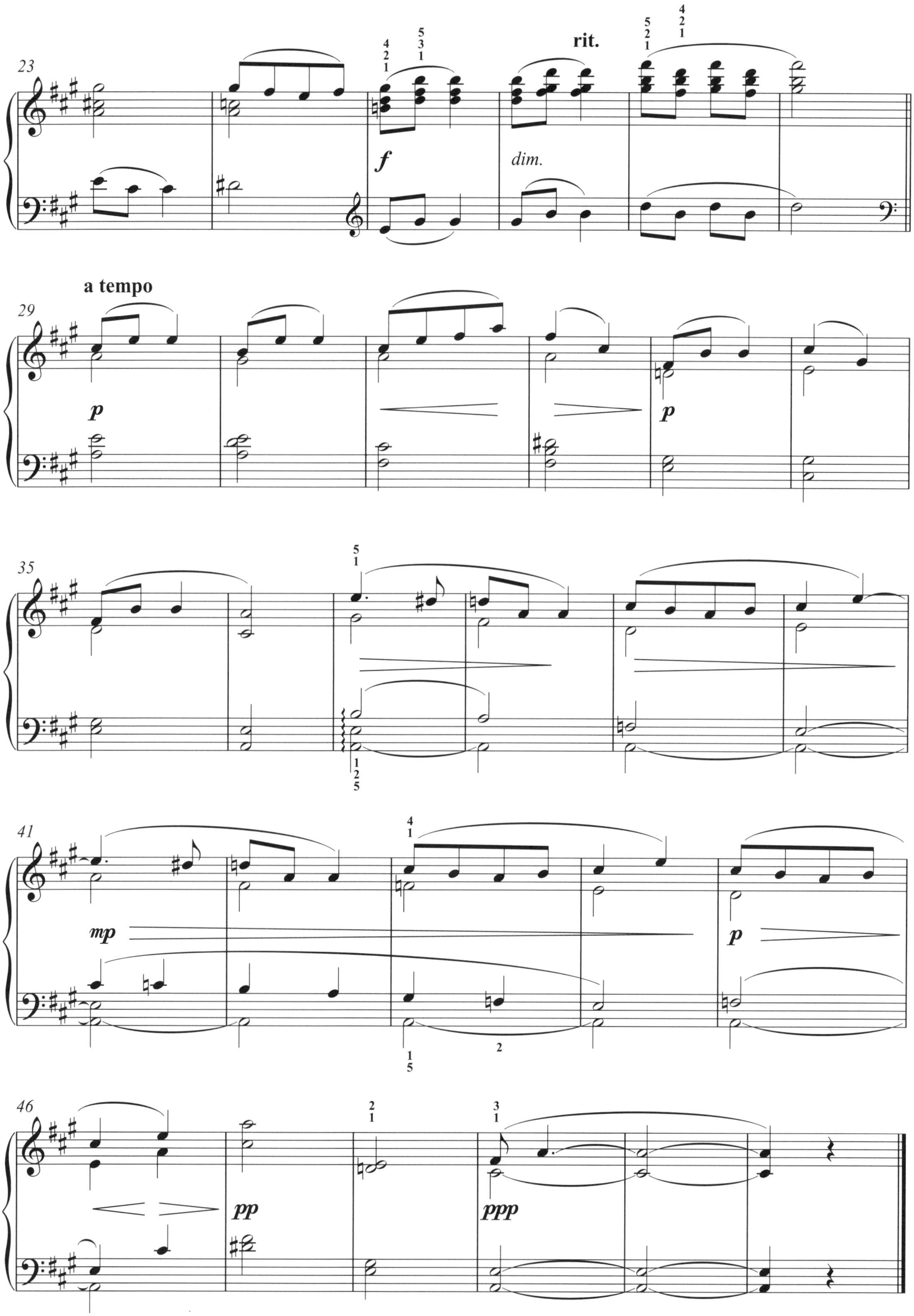
rit.
dim.
a tempo

Uptown Funk!

*Words & Music by Rudy Taylor, Robert Wilson, Lonnie Simmons, Ronnie Wilson, Mark Ronson
Philip Lawrence, Jeffrey Bhasker, Peter Hernandez, Charles Wilson, Nicholaus Williams & Devon Gallaspy*

There are some tricky offbeat rhythms in this piece. Listening to the song will help you get into the groove. Start quietly and build up to a loud finish.

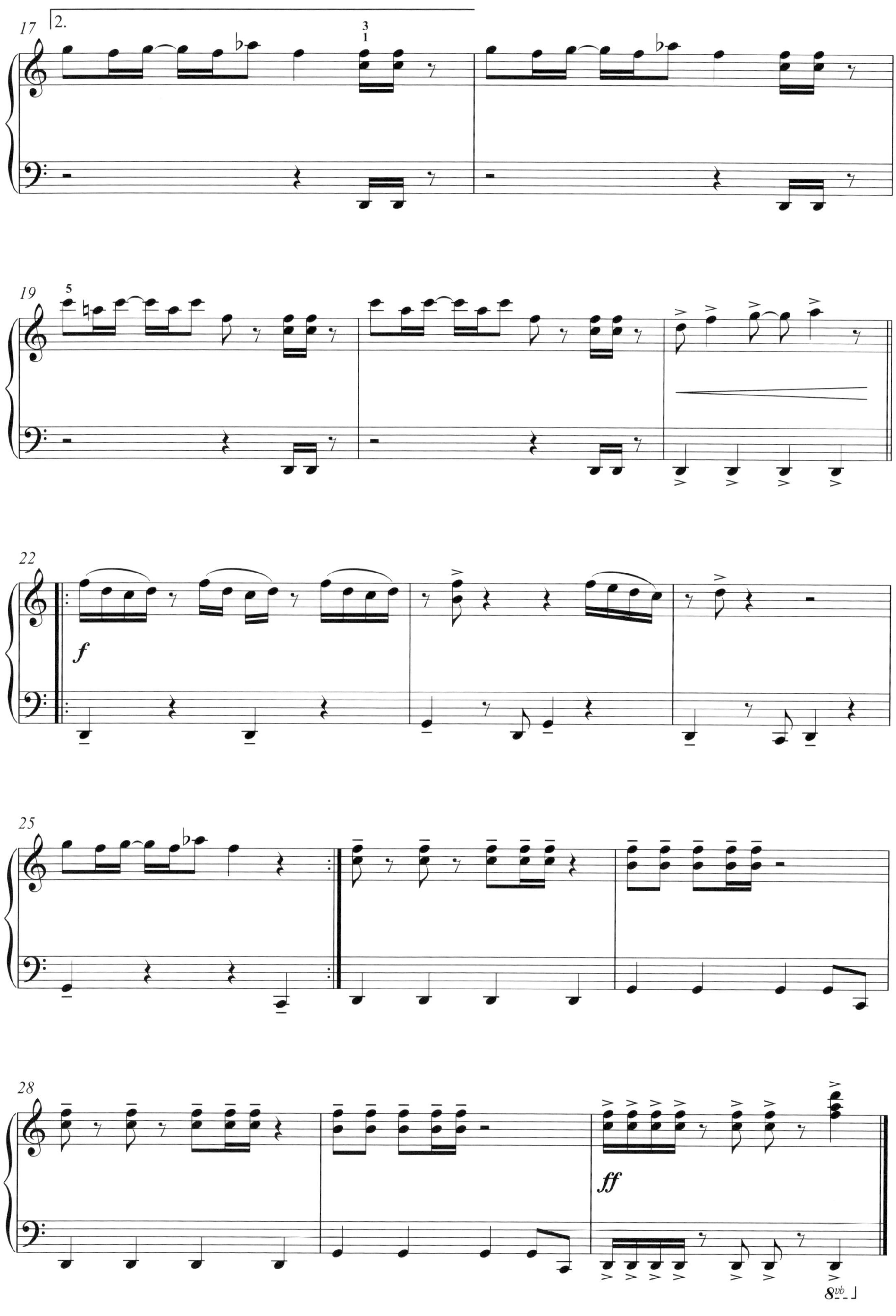

1 2 3 4 5 6 7 8 9

Graded Piano Solos

The 16 pieces in these books have been specially arranged to provide enjoyable supplementary repertoire for pianists. Each piece has been adapted to fit within the specifications of the major exam board grades, and each book covers a wide range of styles, from classical and jazz pieces to contemporary pop.

More Grade 1 Piano Solos
Including:
Chasing Pavements; Hit The Road Jack;
A Whole New World
CH85239

More Grade 2 Piano Solos
Including:
Back To Black; Jurassic Park;
You've Got A Friend In Me
CH85250

More Grade 3 Piano Solos
Including:
Ave Maria; Frozen Heart; Hello;
Writing's On The Wall
CH85261

Grade 2 Piano Solos
Including:
All Of Me; Eine Kleine
Nachtmusik; Let It Go
CH83633

Grade 4 Piano Solos
Including:
Air On The G String; Make You
Feel My Love; Summertime
CH83655

Grade 1 Piano Solos
Including:
Amazing Grace; Lean On Me;
Do You Want To Build A Snowman?
CH83622

Grade 3 Piano Solos
Including:
Für Elise; The Snow Prelude No. 3;
Someone Like You
CH83644

Grade 5 Piano Solos
Including:
Bridge Over Troubled Water;
I Giorni; Take Five
CH83666